Was 9/11 a Movie?

DEAN T. HARTWELL

Available at Amazon.com and other retail stores

Cover illustration drawn by Nicemonkey and courtesy of fotolia

OTHER BOOKS BY DEAN T. HARTWELL

Truth Matters: How the Voters Can Take Back Their Nation

Dead Men Talking: Consequences of Government Lies

Planes without Passengers: The Faked Hijackings of 9/11

Facts Talk but the Guilty Walk: The 9/11 No Hijacker Theory and Its Indictment of Our Leaders

Planes without Passengers: The Faked Hijackings of 9/11 (2nd Edition)

A Fan's Folklore: Six Seasons of Triumph, Tragedy and Tough Luck

St. Peter's Choice: A Novel

Rumors Fly, Truth Walks: How Lies Become Our History

Questions I Wasn't Supposed to Ask

Hartwellbooks.weebly.com
DeanHartwell.weebly.com

ACKNOWLEDGEMENTS

Thank you to all of the 9/11 researchers who have thought outside the box. You know who you are.

Table of Contents

Dean T. Hartwell

PREFACE

I have specialized in the study of evidence of the existence of passengers and planes alleged in the 9/11 event—American 11, American 77, United 93, and United 175.

I have proposed a number of different theories, some of which alluded to passengers taking two of the flights and landing later, either as dupes or as agents of the plot. These theories are laid out in the books *Planes without Passengers: The Faked Hijackings of 9/11*, 1st and 2nd editions.

Thanks to feedback given to me in response to my Scribd.com article "Planes without Passengers Challenge," I came to believe that no one boarded any of the four alleged flights.

I have kept within my theory the possibility that one of the planes, United 175, landed in Cleveland. But there are other reasonable possibilities for the landing place of this flight.

I am still convinced something unusual took place in Cleveland, and I go into detail in particular in this book about a public discussion of a flight to Cleveland by the mayor and members of the national media. The mayor's original statement and the response by United Airlines so contradicted the official story that the plotters had to use damage control to further their deception of the public.

Much of my theory is taken from the first two editions of *Planes without Passengers* and *Dead Men Talking: Consequences of Government Lies*, *Rumors Fly, Truth Walks: Lies Become Our History*, and *Questions I Wasn't Supposed to Ask*. The latter two books discuss 9/11 along with other acts of government deceptions.

Wanting to give my readers a more complete picture of the day's events, I have used now gone into greater detail than before to cover the planes and passengers. But, unlike in previous works, I now also take on as many reasonable questions as I can about all facets of 9/11 rather than limiting my scope to the planes and passengers.

The conclusion may well shock some people and infuriate others. But I ask the reader to judge the facts and not the emotional repercussions of confrontation with new information that contradicts the original belief.

Some may reasonably ask why, after a number of books on this topic, I have decided to publish a new one. Here are my reasons:

I write this book to undo misinformation and misquotes. I aim to re-frame the investigation so as to dismantle presumptions that have been previously made and point out what questions should have been asked all along.

I write this book to give those, like me, who have questioned conventional wisdom, a place to rest, away from the largely uneducated debate that has predominated the discussion of this topic.

I write this book to maintain an open mind on my work by understanding that true research is ongoing. Over time, I have discarded my original presumptions because the evidence I learned far outweighed the old belief and publishing it keeps my ideas transparent.

I write this book to recognize that mistakes that I and others have made no longer bother me. My theory of 9/11 must change when I realize these mistakes and sharing not just what I have learned and how I have learned it is important to me.

I write this book to document my new findings and to further detail what I continue to believe. I have gathered information from different sources and put them all into one place here.

I write this book to challenge critics to cross-examine what I have to say.

I write this book for my longtime readers. Those who have read extensively about the events of 9/11 and those who are new to this topic will learn something from these pages.

One word that will come up frequently is the word "fact." A fact is "something known to exist or to have happened."[1]

How do we know anything?

We know what we see in front of us. We know our names. We know Abraham Lincoln existed.

But what is our knowledge based upon?

Each of these three examples of knowledge rely heavily upon we have been told. I have been told that this object in front of me is a

---

[1] "fact" *The American Heritage® Dictionary of Idioms by Christine Ammer.* Houghton Mifflin Company. 14 Jun. 2015. <Dictionary.com http://dictionary.reference.com/browse/fact>

computer screen. I learned this from my parents.

The same people also told me my name. I never thought to question it because no one else appeared to be questioning their names.

My teachers in school and authors in books I have read have assured me that Abraham Lincoln existed. I know this to be true based heavily on their knowledge, though no person alive now existed during the lifetime of Lincoln.

The funny thing about knowledge is that I also "knew" that 19 hijackers took over airplanes and crashed them into buildings on September 11. I believed this was a fact. But now I do not.

This book may challenge your knowledge of facts, of what truth is or isn't and what truth was or wasn't.

A "debate" over what really happened on this day has been going on since then and all sides in the debate claim to have the facts.

Most disagreement with the official theory has been over who ordered the hijackings, the incompetence of the air defense and whether the United States government had foreknowledge of the events.

For the most part, this "debate" has had little to do with facts, but have instead revolved around articles of faith about the leaders of the United States as to how we understand or come to know facts. Examples abound on the issue of what took place at the Pentagon alone.

Discussion of whether a plane actually struck the Pentagon pitted a group of people who insisted American 77 struck the Pentagon against a group of people the first group derided as "no planers."[2]

This discussion should have been about the obvious outcomes of such a crash. Debaters could have both spoken on whether plane parts that could be proven to have been part of the plane had been found.

Specific questions should have included: Is this how a real Boeing 757 plane crash site would look? Are pieces of planes found at the crash site verifiable parts of the plane that crashed?

The two sides could also have talked about how American 77 or any other plane could have gotten through the Pentagon defense system. Instead, the loudest comment was in the form of a question: "So what happened to

___

[2] https://goo.gl/zwukE1

Barbara Olson and the others who died on those aircraft?"[3]

This question, like others, was reasonable. But this book will provide context for the reader to understand questions that could and should be asked prior to this question so as to better provide an answer for it.

We should ask first whether Barbara Olson boarded any airplane that day. We should also ask where she was as the day started (as she is reported to have taken an early flight). We should ask whether there is any evidence of her or the other "passengers" walking around at the airport or standing at a gate or driving them to the airport to begin with!

The logical order of the question as to what happened to Olson and other passengers is sometime after answers to these questions.

As noted, these and other discussions included large doses of *ad hoc* statements and sarcasm. They also featured insinuations about the rights of victims and patriotism.

Some of my critics have told me not to "insult"[4] the victims of the "tragedy" of 9/11 by

---

[3] http://goo.gl/2qYkGZ
[4] ibid

questioning whether there were passengers. But that presents a problem:

How would I know if there were any passengers or victims if I did not ask questions?

Funny how I never get an answer to this question. Perhaps the question is completely out of the context of knowledge that most people have about the world around us! This book aims to expand that context to include questions previously not asked.

Other terms have popped up frequently, like the phrase "conspiracy theorist." I have explained to those who use the term in a derogatory manner that conspiracy simply means two or more people agreeing to commit a crime.

Criminals, like bank robbers, frequently cannot commit the crime alone. They need assistance from drivers and look out people. So it is with other criminal conduct. In short, *conspiracies take place every day*.

In fact, the official theory about 9/11 posits the conspiracy of Osama bin Laden agreeing with several terrorists to a plan where the terrorists were to hijack planes and fly them into buildings.

When I disagree with the official story put out by our government and our media, I present an *alternative theory*.

We need to get back to discussing facts about this event. And discussing facts is not that difficult. We do it all the time.

Have you ever been involved in a traffic accident? When you talked to your insurance carrier, was your honesty questioned regarding whether the accident actually happened? It is more likely you talked about the facts: the color of the light, the direction you traveled in, when you saw the other car, etc.

The avoidance of questions is a purely conscious decision. If we have already made public statements on a matter, we might find it near impossible to admit that we were wrong.

Are you ready to question what you thought you knew?

Dean T. Hartwell

INTRODUCTION

The events of 9/11 constituted the worst terrorist attack on United States soil in its history. At the orders of Osama bin Laden, nineteen hijackers boarded four different planes, American 11, American 77, United 93 and United 175, killed pilots and passengers and took control of those planes. They then used the planes as weapons to knock down the Twin Towers of the World Trade Center in New York, the Pentagon in Virginia and very nearly the Capitol Building in Washington, D.C.

In one flight, United 93, a brave passenger named Todd Beamer teamed with other passengers to force the plane to crash in a remote area away from the public. In another flight, American 77, Barbara Olson, wife of the Solicitor General of the United States, called her husband to ask for help on what to do about a hijacking on her flight.

That is the official version of events. Every successful candidate for high office in the United States has affirmed their belief in this story line, with the mainstream media rarely challenging them and instead allowing their mediums of communication to be used as a platform for our leaders to say the story.

Was 9/11 a Movie? will provide grounds for the reader to ask relevant questions about the official story so that they make their own decision as to what really happened.

Much of the official story came from those who alleged receiving phone calls from passengers using cell phones on these flights.

This should come as no surprise. Without the fake calls, we would have no reports of hijackers, knives, box cutters, red bandanas, imminent plane crashes, etc. Who would our leaders have blamed for what happened? This is where our leaders got their "terrorists" for their "war on terror" story.

Veteran 9/11 researcher David Ray Griffin cites a number of mainstream media sources that reported shortly after 9/11 calls from the planes as cell phone calls and notes that the FBI did not object, at least not publicly.[5]

The FBI, confronted by evidence from AK Dewdney and others that cell phone calls do not work on planes in flight, provided a new official version of the calls by labeling all but

---

[5] http://goo.gl/oP8EMt

two of them calls from air phones in a report for the Zacarias Moussaoui trial in 2006.

This book will delve into those alleged phone calls and how knowledge of the calls became part of the official story.

At the Moussaoui trial, the prosecution and the defense both stipulated to the phone call findings. That is to say, they never debated the veracity of the calls or the phone records, meaning that we cannot use the court system to determine whether the calls really took place.

These are only a few of the problems with the use of the alleged phone calls to promote any story, not just the official one.

Here is the order of this book:

The reader will review the official theories of each of the four alleged flights in the chapter entitled "Flights 11, 75, 93 and 175" with the aid of timelines. My factual assertions regarding issues raised follow each of the official theories in order to distinguish my own point of view and to provide framework for later discussion.

The flights are listed in numerical order for easy reference. I also wished to unburden the reader from presumption of the official theory merely because it asserts that flight happened in a particular order. Each flight is a story in its own right and can be analyzed both individually and as part of an overall story.

The middle of this book focuses upon my search for the flights, passengers and phone calls. New assertions of fact, based upon issues that the official theory does not sufficiently cover, receive analysis. There is a special chapter about Barbara Olson and Todd Beamer, two passengers who have received heavy media attention, here. Alleged phone calls on each flight receive their own timelines.

A new timeline that depicts both official and alternative theory assertions comes up next.

The book then goes to a chapter called "Ask the Right Questions." By this point, the reader will have heard competing theories and competing assertions of fact. The question and answer format provides my most definitive answer to every question for which I have an answer.

All the facts in the world are of no help unless they relate to one another. The title chapter "Was 9/11 a Movie?" fits in here to create a new story about the day's events to explain the facts in a manner that all readers can appreciate and understand.

In concluding, I surmise the chances of society accepting this theory of 9/11. It does not look so good at the moment.

By the end of the book, the reader will see a new way to "frame" the events of that day. Consideration of the idea that those events were staged and scripted like a movie will provide "glasses" for the reader to see clearly what looked blurry before.

Dean T. Hartwell

FLIGHTS 11, 77, 93 AND 175

Dean T. Hartwell

AMERICAN 11 OFFICIAL TIMELINE

Various sources are used for this and the other flight timelines. These sources include media sources quoting authorities, transcripts of air traffic controllers and documents prepared by officials.[6]

7:40 AM—Boston, Logan Airport. Ninety-two people, including 11 crew members, board American 11, a Boeing 767-223ER with tail number N334AA.[7] The flight destination is Los Angeles.[8]

7:59 AM—American 11 takes off from runway 4-R.

8:13 AM—The pilots' last radio communication is made from the pilots to ground control: "twenty right American eleven."[9]

8:15 AM—Boston Air Traffic Control begins unsuccessful attempts to contact the pilots

---

[6] Many footnotes use a shortened form of the URL so as to maintain neatness and save space. The reader is encouraged to check these notes.

[7] http://en.wikipedia.org/wiki/American_Airlines_Flight_11

[8] http://goo.gl/1SejxY

[9] http://goo.gl/ZrGgfP

after the plane fails to respond to an order to climb.[10]

8:20 AM—American 11 stops transmitting its transponder signal and veers northward and departs dramatically from the westward heading of its planned route. The controllers conclude that the plane has probably been hijacked.[11]

8:24 AM—The following transmission is reportedly received from Flight 11:

> *We have some planes. Just stay quiet and you'll be okay ... we are returning to the airport.*
>
> *...Nobody move. Everything will be okay. If you try to make any moves, you'll endanger yourself and the airplane. Just stay quiet.*
>
> *Nobody move please we are going back to the airport ... don't try to make any stupid moves.*[12]

---

[10] http://goo.gl/2Gsu5o
[11] http://goo.gl/x3oiak
[12] http://goo.gl/sA0zlb

Neither of the pilots press the distress call button. (In fact, no report of any distress calls would come from any of the alleged flights.)

8:28 AM—controllers reportedly watch the plane make a 100-degree turn toward the south.[13]

During the flight, five hijackers take over the aircraft by breaching the cockpit. Two of the flight attendants, Amy Sweeney and Betty Ong, make calls to American Airlines and report the hijacking and injuries to passengers. The Ong call was tape recorded, with a portion of it made available to the public.

8:46 AM—The plane crashes into the World Trade Center (north tower), killing everyone on board.

Aftermath—Firefighters and rescue workers find human remains at the World Trade Center and the immediate area[14] and within a year medical examiners declare that the remains matched DNA samples given by the passengers' families.[15] A copy[16] of the manifest

---

[13] http://goo.gl/iuCaEz
[14] http://goo.gl/l9CGk5
[15] http://goo.gl/IM3mjV
[16] http://911research.wtc7.net/planes/evidence/docs/Flight11.png

shows the names of passengers who took the flight.

FACTS ABOUT AMERICAN 11

1. Flight 11 never took off on September 11, 2001.

The Bureau of Transportation Statistics (BTS)[17] originally did not show American Airlines Flights 11 and 77 as having been scheduled or having taken off on September 11, 2001. The late researcher Gerard Holmgren identified this fact and made it public on November 13, 2003.[18]

By 2004, the BTS records showed something completely different about these flights. The new explanation said the following:

On September 11, 2001, American Airlines Flight #11 and #77 and United Airlines #93 and #175 were hijacked by terrorists. Therefore,

---

[17] The airline ontime performance data portion of the BTS "contains on-time arrival data for non-stop domestic flights by major air carriers, and provides such additional items as departure and arrival delays, origin and destination airports, flight numbers, scheduled and actual departure and arrival times, cancelled or diverted flights, taxi-out and taxi-in times, air time, and non-stop distance." See http://goo.gl/Heeca - the omission of American 11 and 77 is glaring.

[18] Hendrie, Edward. *9/11: Enemies Foreign and Domestic*; Great Mountain Publishing; Garrisonville VA; 2011; 9. See also http://thewebfairy.com/holmgren/1177.html

these flights are not included in the on-time summary statistics.[19]

BTS records were filed contemporaneously with the events of that day. This evidence is highly significant because it (1) involves records routinely kept by a government agency that (2) were unaccountably altered in a way that appears to cover up a fact incongruent with the official story.

The reliability of this evidence makes it one of the first things a real investigation would have looked at in studying the case.

The alteration of evidence suggests the consciousness of guilt, and the availability of the original records to the public has been hampered by those with the duty to reveal them.

2. The official story cannot be specific about where the take-off occurred.

Furthermore, the official story cannot pinpoint the boarding gate as Gate 26 or Gate 32. Nor has any relative or friend of any of the "passengers" of any "flight" identified themselves as the one who drove the "passenger" to the airport or waited with them

---

[19] http://goo.gl/vxIL4

at the boarding gate. Perhaps these relatives or friends could have been questioned about which gate they went to. Inconsistencies could establish an element of fiction in the story of Flight 11.

Confirming this type of information would have been a top priority in a true investigation.

3. Where were the remains of the passengers?

No source independent of the government has identified remains of any of the flight's passengers. As elements in the government were complicit in tampering with the flight records, how can elements of the government be trusted with the so-called DNA samples?

The key to DNA samples is that evidence of the chain of custody must be shown to be conclusive.

DNA testing requires a sample from a victim at the "scene" and a sample from the victim or a close relative from somewhere else (usually given by family).

An agent (of the plot) would likely retrieve a sample from the "scene" of the victim's death.

The agent would give samples to the tester. (The tester, as one who would follow standard procedures, would not have any reason to go to the scene nor to question the agent.)

The agent would also go to the family to ask for samples (e.g., hair, toothbrush, etc.).

The agent would then give the family sample to the tester.

If the tester were in on the plot, the tests could be easily rigged. But the tester's statements to the media are needed. If something "happened" to the tester, it would cause too much suspicion. The tester would be suspicious if "scene" samples did not have the appearance of involvement in a plane crash.

Respected 9/11 researcher Elias Davidsson[20] points to a lack of a "chain of custody." This is a legal principle which directs those who investigate a crime to document (1) how and where they find evidence and (2) how the evidence got to the point of the hearing.

He states that "there is no indication that a proper chain of custody between the crash sites and the final disposition of bodily remains had been established by the FBI, as required

---

[20] http://goo.gl/hij3bk

in criminal cases. The 9/11 Commission did not refer to any such documentation."[21]

With no solid chain of custody, a prosecutor (the state) can conceivably bring just about any piece of evidence to the attention of the jury. And when the public is the jury with no judge to referee, the state can use this opportunity to perpetuate a false story.

4. There is no proof of boarding.

Davidsson names the evidence that the government should have revealed if it really had a case that could be proven as to the people that boarded the planes:

In order to prove that particular individuals actually boarded the aircrafts and died at the known crash sites, at least three types of evidence could and should have been produced: Authenticated passenger lists (or flight manifests) displaying their names, identification of the suspects as they boarded the aircraft, and identification of their bodily remains from the crash sites.

I only disagree with Davidsson as to the identification of the "suspects" as I now believe there were no hijackers. If it could be

---

[21] http://newcrisispapers.com/noevidence.pdf

established a hijacking took place, the issue would be relevant.

In short, the "evidence" of remains of "passengers" from Flight 11, and with the other three flights, would most likely fail in a contested case in a court of law.

Furthermore, what some refer to as "manifests" simply refer to lists of passengers brought up at the aforementioned Moussaoui trial five years after the events of 9/11. It is worthwhile to ask where these "manifests" had been for that time and why we should consider them to be authentic. Previous lists of passengers were provided by the media shortly after the day. The media has never been forthright as to how they obtained those lists.

5. Information about the plane parts does not add up.

No debris from the scene at the World Trade Center has ever been traced by serial number to the plane that allegedly flew on 9/11 as Flight 11.[22]

Put another way, every part of each airplane has a serial number on the part that identifies several things about the part such as when it is

---

[22] http://physics911.net/georgenelson/

time for that part to be replaced and which specific plane that part is on.

The identification of this and the other planes is paramount to understanding what happened and should have been on the list of things for the investigators to find out. Leaving this information out is like a murder investigation failing to identify the murder weapon!

AMERICAN 77 OFFICIAL TIMELINE

7:50 AM—Washington, Dulles Airport. Sixty-four people, including the five crew members, boarded American 77 at Gate D26.

8:20 AM—The flight, a Boeing 757-223 with tail number N644AA, takes off from Runway 30 with Los Angeles as its destination.[23]

8:46 AM—Flight 77 veers severely off course.

8:50 AM—The last normal radio communication was made from the pilots and air traffic control.

8:55 AM—The plane begins to turn south.

8:56 AM—The jet's transponder is shut off.[24] The pilots' last transmission is unusual. The pilots is reported to have said "ah direct FALMOUTH American seventy seven thanks." No radio communications from the flight indicate distress.[25]

9:00 AM—The plane begins to head east. Shortly thereafter it begins to descend from its

---

[23] http://en.wikipedia.org/wiki/American_Airlines_Flight_77
[24] http://goo.gl/9lrPS
[25] http://goo.gl/u7R09E

altitude of 35,000 feet. The autopilot is engaged and disengaged multiple times.

9:29 AM—The plane is now 35 miles west of the Pentagon, flying at 7,000 feet.

9:34 AM—The plane is now about 3.5 miles west-southwest of the Pentagon and starts a 330-degree descending right turn, bringing it to an altitude of about 2,000 feet four miles southwest of the Pentagon.[26]

During the flight, five hijackers take over the aircraft and force the passengers to the back of the aircraft. Some of the passengers, including famed political commentator Barbara Olson, make calls to family members.

9:37 AM—The plane crashes into the west side of the Pentagon at 9:37 AM, killing everyone on board and 125 people who were in the building.[27]

Aftermath—Investigators find human remains at the Pentagon and the immediate area and declare that the remains matched DNA samples given by the passengers' families. A

---

[26] Ibid.
[27] http://en.wikipedia.org/wiki/American_Airlines_Flight_77

copy of the manifest[28] shows the names of the passengers who took the flight.

---

[28] http://911research.wtc7.net/planes/evidence/docs/Flight77.png

FACTS ABOUT AMERICAN 77

1. American 77 never took off on September 11, 2001.

As noted above for American Flight 11, the Bureau of Transportation Statistics (BTS) originally did not show American Airlines Flights 11 and 77 as having been scheduled or having taken off (wheels off) on September 11, 2001. The late researcher Gerard Holmgren identified this fact and made it public on November 13, 2003.[29]

By 2004, the BTS records showed something completely different about these flights. The new explanation said the following:

On September 11, 2001, American Airlines Flight #11 and #77 and United Airlines #93 and #175 were hijacked by terrorists. Therefore, these flights are not included in the on-time summary statistics.[30]

---

[29] Hendrie, ibid.
[30] http://goo.gl/vxIL4

2. No one is reported to have said they saw anyone board this plane.

Researcher Elias Davidsson asked American Airlines for permission to interview employees who saw the passengers off, but the airlines denied the request on the grounds of privacy.[31] What was American Airlines hiding?

Or perhaps the airlines were directed by authority (i.e. government officials) not to release this information. In either case, an investigation with subpoena authority could and should pursue these interviews, especially given that other means of corroborating the presence of passengers are suspect. See the next issue.

3. There were no remains proven to be from the passengers.

No source independent of the government has identified remains of any of the flight's passengers. See the discussion of DNA in the American 11 section earlier.

---

[31] Davidsson, Elias. *Hijacking America's Mind on 9/11: Counterfeiting Evidence*; Algora Publishing; New York; 2013; 47.

4. The plane parts do not add up.

No debris from the scene at the Pentagon has ever been traced by serial number to the plane that allegedly flew on 9/11 as Flight 77.[32]

No plane part in the debris at the Pentagon scene has ever been traced by the serial number on the part to the plane that allegedly flew on 9/11 as Flight 77.

In the words of Col. George Nelson, USAF (ret.), had United 93 crashed in Shanksville "there would have [been] literally hundreds of serially-controlled time-change parts within the hole that would have proved beyond any shadow of doubt the precise tail-number or identity of the aircraft."[33]

---

[32] http://physics911.net/georgenelson/
[33] Ibid.

UNITED 93 OFFICIAL TIMELINE

8:00 AM—Forty-four people, including seven crew members, board United 93, a Boeing 757-200 with registration number N591UA at gate A17 at Newark International Airport.[34]

8:28 AM—The flight took off from Newark Airport with San Francisco as its destination (Source: Bureau of Transportation Statistics).[35]

8:42 AM—The flight took off from Newark Airport with San Francisco as its destination (according to mainstream sources).[36]

9:16 AM—The FAA informs North American Aerospace Defense Command (NORAD) that the flight may have been hijacked.

9:27 AM—Several communications with air traffic controllers later indicate that Flight 93 is hijacked at around this time.[37]

[**Author's comment**: the reader may note an eleven minute difference between the FAA telling NORAD and traffic controllers learning

---

[34] http://en.wikipedia.org/wiki/United_Airlines_Flight_93
[35] https://goo.gl/Vp7S45
[36] Ibid.
[37] http://www.cnn.com/2001/US/09/16/inv.hijack.warning/

of the hijacking. It may call into question the reliability of the reports!]

9:30 AM—The transponder signal ceases. At about this time, the plane apparently reverses direction and begins flying toward the capital.[38]

During the flight, four hijackers take over the aircraft. After making calls from the airplane to relatives, several passengers rush the hijackers in an attempt to wrest control of the plane back.

10:03 AM—The plane crashes in a field in Shanksville, Pennsylvania, killing everyone on board.[39]

Aftermath—Investigators found human remains in Shanksville and declared that the remains matched DNA samples given by the passengers' families. Copies of the manifest[40] and boarding passes[41] show the names of the passengers who took the flight.

---

[38] http://911research.wtc7.net/planes/attack/flight93.html
[39] http://en.wikipedia.org/wiki/United_Airlines_Flight_93
[40] http://911research.wtc7.net/planes/evidence/docs/Flight93.png
[41] http://goo.gl/GwPkXW

FACTS ABOUT UNITED 93

1. United 93 flew well beyond the time we are told it crashed.

The flight was airborne over Champaign, Illinois, at the same time as its alleged crash in Shanksville. It is identified clearly by the Airplane Communications and Reporting System (ACARS) as N591UA.[42]

2. The county coroner could not find evidence of passengers at the "crash" site.

Wallace Miller, Coroner of Somerset County (which includes Shanksville) and one of the first to arrive at the "crash" scene, said of the area, "This is the most eerie thing. I have not, to this day, eleven months later seen a single drop of blood. Not a drop."[43]

Miller also reportedly said that "Usually you see much debris, wreckage, and much noise and commotion. This crash was different. There was no wreckage, no bodies, and no noise. ... It appeared as though there were no

---

[42] http://pilotsfor911truth.org/MORE-ACARS-CONFIRMATION.html
[43] http://goo.gl/xVjqrT

passengers or crew on this plane (as told to author David McCall).[44]

   3. No one can prove there were any remains from passengers.

No source independent of our government, which has an obvious conflict of interest in this matter, has identified remains of any of the flight's passengers.

---

[44] http://www.whale.to/b/flight_9323.html

UNITED 175 OFFICIAL TIMELINE

8:14 AM—At Boston's Logan Airport, 65 people, including nine crew members, board from Terminal C's Gate 19 United 175, a Boeing 767-222 with registration number N612UA.[45]

8:14 AM—The flight takes off from runway 9 with Los Angeles as its destination.

8:41 AM—A United 175 pilot reports that he has overheard a transmission (presumably from by-then-hijacked Flight 11):

> *ya we figured we'd wait to go to you center ah we heard a suspicious transmission on our departure out of Boston ah with someone ah, ah sound like someone sound like someone keyed the mike and said ah everyone ah stay in your seats.*

Shortly thereafter, the last radio communication is made from the pilots and air traffic control: "that's ah cut out ... did you copy that?"[46]

---

[45] http://en.wikipedia.org/wiki/United_Airlines_Flight_175
[46] http://nsarchive.gwu.edu/NSAEBB/NSAEBB196/doc03.pdf

8:42 AM—United 175 veers off its planned course and begins flying south.[47]

8:43 AM—The FAA notifies NORAD that the flight had been hijacked.[48]

8:46 AM—United 175 stops transmitting its transponder signal.[49]

During the flight, five hijackers take over the aircraft and breach the cockpit and take over the controls. Some of the passengers make calls to family members.

9:03 AM—United 175 strikes World Trade Center south tower, killing all aboard.[50]

Aftermath—Investigators find human remains at the World Trade Center and the immediate area and declare that the remains matched DNA samples given by the passengers' families. A copy of the manifest[51] shows the names of the passengers who took the flight.

---

[47] http://goo.gl/9lrPS
[48] http://911research.wtc7.net/planes/attack/flight175.html
[49] http://www.theguardian.com/world/2001/oct/17/september11.usa
[50] http://en.wikipedia.org/wiki/United_Airlines_Flight_175
[51] http://911research.wtc7.net/planes/evidence/docs/Flight175.png

FACTS ABOUT UNITED 175

1. United 175 flew well longer than was officially reported.

United 175 flew over Harrisburg, Pennsylvania, 15 minutes after it allegedly hit the World Trade Center.[52] As with Flight 93, ACARS messages were sent to Flight 175 that indicate that the plane was heading far away from its "crash" scene. Pilots for 9/11 Truth discovered that Flight 175 was tracked in western Pennsylvania several minutes after it allegedly struck the World Trade Center. The plane is identified clearly as N612UA.[53]

2. No one can prove there were any remains from passengers at the "crash" site.

No source independent of the government has identified remains of any of the flight's passengers.

---

[52] http://pilotsfor911truth.org/ACARS-CONFIRMED-911-AIRCRAFT-AIRBORNE-LONG-AFTER-CRASH.html
[53] http://pilotsfor911truth.org/ACARS-CONFIRMED-911-AIRCRAFT-AIRBORNE-LONG-AFTER-CRASH.html

3. The plane parts do not add up.

No debris from the scene at the World Trade Center has ever been traced by serial number to the plane that allegedly flew on 9/11 as Flight 175.[54]

---

[54] http://physics911.net/georgenelson/

Dean T. Hartwell

THE SEARCH FOR FLIGHTS

Dean T. Hartwell

There are Conflicting Stories about the "Black Boxes"

There have been conflicting reports about the black boxes (which include cockpit voice recorders and flight data recorders that record the last thirty minutes of a plane's voices and noises) recovered.

The *9/11 Commission Report* states, "the cockpit voice recorders and flight data recorders from American 11 and United 175 were not found."[55] This result is extremely unusual.[56]

In fact, the *Philadelphia Daily News* said that "Federal aviation officials—blaming the massive devastation—have said the World Trade Center attacks seem to be the only major jetliner crashes in which the critical devices were never located."[57]

But *Counterpunch* magazine reported on December 19, 2005, that sources have said the FBI actually has these boxes from both

---

[55] *9/11 Commission Report,* chapter 1, footnote 76.
[56] Morgan, Rowland and Ian Henshall. *9/11 Revealed – Unanswered Questions*; Carroll & Graf Publishers, New York, 2005, 115
[57] http://goo.gl/wsqs07

flights.[58] No official has yet commented on the tapes or revealed their contents.[59]

Voice recorders were discovered for Flights 77 and 93. However, the Flight 77 voice recorder was deemed unreadable,[60] a highly unusual conclusion!

Officials found the black box for United 93. But there is no doubt that the last three minutes of the cockpit voice recording are missing.[61] Missing portions of a cockpit voice recordings are also highly unusual!

The government has refused to admit to this discrepancy, leading me to believe that something is missing from the tape, which ends with passengers yelling frantically and apparent hijackers alternating shouting, "Cut off the oxygen" and "Allah is the greatest."[62]

What could have happened during the missing three minutes that followed? What secret could the government be hiding?

---

[58] http://goo.gl/TLLs0z
[59] http://goo.gl/ilvWxh
[60] http://en.wikipedia.org/wiki/List_of_unrecovered_flight_recorders
[61] http://www.911review.org/Wiki/Flight93.shtml
[62] http://goo.gl/9TruF8

Or are these unusual events proof that there really was no "black box"?

Alice Hoagland, the mother of alleged United 93 victim Mark Bingham, made an interesting observation. The FBI agreed to play the tape for her and other family members of victims, and she reported hearing a voice at the very end of the tape which said, "Pull it up" in a calm, fluent English speaking voice.[63]

The black boxes could tell us where a given plane actually went and confirm which ones did not fly. The black boxes really are missing, someone with high enough authority has ordered that they not see the light of day or perhaps these boxes never existed.

FAA Response Sounds Scripted to "Miss" the Planes

No officials scrambled any planes to intercept the "hijacked" planes until it was far too late to stop them. A good investigation would ask why not.

The Federal Aviation Administration could have acted on its own to scramble planes to intercept and, in fact, did so on 67 occasions in

---

[63] Morgan and Henshall, *9/11 Revealed*, p. 154

the one-year period before 9/11.[64] In a well-known case, the FAA contacted the military immediately when the FAA confirmed that an airplane carrying professional golfer Payne Stewart went off course in 1999.

But Vice President Cheney stated to Tim Russert on *Meet the Press* on September 16, 2001, that "the toughest decision was this question of whether we [the White House] would intercept incoming aircraft."[65] He gave viewers the distinct impression that intercepting meant shooting down aircraft and that this decision was made at the Presidential level.

He may have misled the public as to who could have scrambled the planes in time to divert the hijackers and as to the appropriate procedure for the FAA to follow. Only the President (or acting President) can authorize a shoot-down. But, again, no presidential approval is needed for an intercept.

In the event of an emergency, the FAA notifies its Air Defense Liaison. This official works in NORAD and coordinates with the United

---

[64] Ruppert, Michael. *Crossing the Rubicon*, New Society Publishers, Gabriola Island, Canada, 2004, p. 309
[65] http://goo.gl/03vjXY

States military to handle emergencies, such as hijackings or airplanes that have clearly deviated from the flight plan the pilots created before take-off.[66]

Some supporters of the official theory contend that the Department of Defense must be notified in the event of a hijacking and that this problem of notification stalled the lines of communication on 9/11. But the policy in force, a memo dated June 1, 2001, and issued by the Chairman of the Joint Chiefs of Staff, titled "Aircraft Piracy and Destruction of Derelict Airborne Objects," states that "immediate responses" are excepted from the rule that supporters cite.[67]

What else could have hampered the FAA response on 9/11? Several sources, including the mainstream media and former Bush Administration counter-terrorism expert Richard Clarke, have identified at least five simulations of war strategy, including a plane hijacking scenario, taking place on 9/11.[68]

---

[66] Ahmed, Nafeez Mosaddeq, *The War on Truth: 9/11, Disinformation, and the Anatomy of Terrorism*. Olive Branch Press, Northampton, MA, 2005, 315.
[67] http://www.dtic.mil/doctrine/jel/cjcsd/cjcsi/3610_01a.pdf
[68] Ruppert, 336.

For example, Operation Northern Vigilance, a war-game simulation, took place in Colorado at the same time that planes allegedly flew into the World Trade Center. This operation simulated long-range bombers poised to strike Alaska and Northern Canada.

The *Toronto Star* reported: "NORAD's Northeast Air Defense Sector (NEADS), based in Rome, N.Y., contacts the mountain. The Federal Aviation Administration has evidence of a hijacking and is asking for NORAD support. This [hijacking] is not a part of the exercise..."[69]

Perhaps this simulation accounts for a 20-minute delay from the time NORAD's northeast branch NEADS learned of the "hijacking" of Flight 175 and the time it alerted NORAD's Command Center.

And a similar occurrence happened with another war-game simulation, Vigilant Guardian (designed to test the network of radar watch systems), when a NORAD commander heard about a hijacking from the FAA at 8:40 AM on the same day. He wondered whether it

---

[69] Ahmed, 305.

was a part of the exercise and learned shortly thereafter that it was not.[70]

Critics of the war-game simulation theory have stated that there were simulations that day, but that none of them affected the tracking of the planes. These critics cite an answer given by then-Chair of Joint Chiefs of Staff Richard Myers to then-Representative Cynthia McKinney. She had asked him "about the four war games that were taking place on September 11 and how they may have impaired our ability to respond to those attacks."

Myers responded by saying that all battle positions were manned because of the drills "…so it was an easy transition from an exercise into a real-world situation. It actually enhanced the response."[71]

But this answer fails to address the statements of the people who had to react to the combined simulations and real planes. According to FAA head Jane Garvey, her team had to contend with as many as 11 planes in the air calling for help at or around the same time.[72] As a result,

[70] Ibid, 304.
[71] http://goo.gl/6Dk9yL
[72] http://goo.gl/Hj9jFm

many at the FAA and Air Force were confused as to which hijackings were real and which were not.

Reports of simulated hijackings flooded the FAA computers to the extent that the FAA employees must have felt like jugglers who started out with a few balls in the air and who kept getting more balls thrown to them. They may have felt unable to form a strategy to determine which hijackings were real and which were not and, thus, could not respond at all.

Some of the air traffic controllers made tape recordings of their reflections shortly after the attacks. These reflections might have given an accurate picture as to what those who saw the screens tried to do in response, but an FAA supervisor destroyed the tapes.[73]

This apparent plan to confuse the FAA required someone with the authority to control the schedule of the war simulations combined with foreknowledge of the attacks on September 11th. The *Cable News Network* may have given us an answer. According to an April 19, 2004,

---

[73] Ruppert, 369

CNN broadcast that cited NORAD sources, the White House knew of the drills.[74]

Given that there were no hijackings at all on September 11, 2001, the plotters engineered the best strategy possible to confuse the officials in charge of tracking hijackings down: delay their response until they showed up too late to see that there was nothing to see!

Eyewitness to United 93 Misquoted

Only United 93 had an eyewitness who reported seeing passengers board firsthand. Then-New York Giant football player Clayton White, according to a newspaper report that can no longer be accessed on the Internet, made a comment about United 93 passengers boarding their plane on the tarmac on which his team's plane landed on September 11, 2001. *Or so I thought.*

White had reportedly made the comment about two weeks later in response to a flight attendant telling him on a subsequent flight into Newark that United 93 took off from that point on September 11. He was shocked and stated

---

[74] Ruppert, 372

that he remembered seeing people board the plane from the tarmac.[75]

The comment suggested that passengers boarded United 93 from an unusual location. It is worth mentioning what he allegedly said because it fits with the idea that whoever boarded this flight would need to avoid official identification that ordinary boarding would encompass.

But hold the presses! I reached now-Coach Clayton White of North Carolina State's football team by telephone on May 26, 2015. He explained to me that "[the writer] didn't have a picture of what I was talking about." When his team flew on a plane two weeks later to Kansas City, he related, it was the first time they had flown since September 11 and the topic came up.

"The Giants charter plane had the same stewardess on all away games." She told him on the Kansas City flight that Flight 93 had been "right beside" their charter plane on 9/11.

White went on to emphasize that he never saw the flight's passengers.

---

[75] http://goo.gl/f5mJ7r

Comments made by another man named White provide more pieces to this puzzle.

Cleveland Mayor White Speaks up, then Clams up, about Flight

A message posted briefly on a radio station's website on the day of September 11, 2001, continues to confound 9/11 researchers today.

The Mayor of Cleveland, Michael R. White, held a press conference at 11:00 AM and reported that a Boeing 767 out of Boston had made an emergency landing in Cleveland because of bomb threats and that it "had been moved to a secure area of the airport and evacuated."

WCPO radio of Cincinnati posted an Associated Press article[76] about 45 minutes later quoting the Mayor and saying that in addition, United had identified the plane as United 93. United was also quoted as saying it was "deeply concerned" about United 175.

As noted earlier, United 93 flew out of Newark and United 175 flew out of Boston that day. United 93 was a Boeing 757, while United 175 was a Boeing 767. Clearly, United 175 fits the

---

[76] http://goo.gl/NuoshQ

description of Mayor White's comments much better than United 93.

The link to the AP article was removed from the website minutes later with the reason given being that it was "factually incorrect." But no explanation was given as to what fact or facts were wrong.

Asking about that fact or facts would have been a good question for a true investigation.

Followers of the official theory will likely say that United 93 had crashed shortly after 10:00 AM that morning. But why wouldn't the site state this as the reason for the correction?

Mayor White would later say that there had been no hijacking nor any bomb found. His office also said the landing was a precaution.[77] At least one researcher has contacted him in the years since and has gotten the reply from White that he no longer does interviews.[78]

---

[77] http://goo.gl/NuoshQ
[78] Hendrie, 37.

When Did the Associated Press Get Information from United Airlines?

Officially, United did not reveal to its own employees, let alone the public, that United 93 had crashed until 10:15 AM. After that point, any communication from United about a bomb threat on Flight 93 would implicitly contradict the official story.

The idea that United 93 flew to Cleveland before White's 11:00 announcement runs into problems as well. With United 93 over Champaign, Illinois at about 10:10 AM, there would be little time for a bomb scare to be acknowledged, sent through the official channels to United and then told in time to Mayor White. And again, United 93 was a Boeing 757, not a 767, and it flew from Newark, not Boston.

It is undisputed that Delta 1989 (a Boeing 767) flew out of Boston, was thought to have a bomb threat, and made an emergency landing in Cleveland at 10:10 AM. But the idea that the Mayor and the AP referred to this flight at 11:00 and said the plan had been evacuated contradicts the newspaper report that Delta

1989 passengers were not evacuated[79] for more than two hours after their landing (at around 12:10 PM).

What Plane Was the Mayor and the AP Talking About?

United 175 took off from Boston five minutes before United 93 took off from Newark (8:23 AM). United 175 was a Boeing 767. As with United 93, ACARS[80] has placed United 175 as flying after its alleged crash. Of course, United is quoted as saying United 93 made the emergency landing and that it was "concerned" about United 175.

ACARS places United 175 over the vicinity[81] of Harrisburg at 8:59 AM. The "mystery" flight at Cleveland landed at 10:45 AM. With a take-off time of 8:14, United 175 would have, by 8:59, have approached its cruising altitude. At cruising speed, a Boeing 767 can go at least 500 miles per hour.[82]

---

[79] http://goo.gl/BDzvLQ

[80] http://pilotsfor911truth.org/ACARS-CONFIRMED-911-AIRCRAFT-AIRBORNE-LONG-AFTER-CRASH.html

[81] ACARS routes messages through remote ground stations similar to the way in which cell phone calls are routed. It does not give an exact location but rather the location of the station used to route the particular message.

[82] http://en.wikipedia.org/wiki/Boeing_767

The flight distance, according to Google, between Harrisburg and Cleveland, measures 331 miles. Given further ACARS information that United 175 flew over Pittsburgh, 203 miles from Harrisburg, at 9:23 AM, it is entirely possible that United 175 could have made it to Cleveland by 10:45 AM.

ACARS shows United 93 over Champaign, Illinois at 9:51 AM. Google shows that Cleveland is 439 miles away. However, United 93 had already gone PAST Cleveland and would have had to make a U-turn to go back east. Such a move would likely have caught the attention of air traffic controllers.

Furthermore, the Federal Aviation Administration order at 10:10 AM for all planes to land immediately would have made a United 93 landing in Cleveland impossible.

So why did United 93 come up in connection with Cleveland?

Hypothesis: Representatives from the AP and United had a conversation that morning before any reports got out about any plane crashes to either employees or the public.

_____

This would explain the reference apparently left in the AP post in which the airline expresses its concern for United 175, whose alleged crash United did not make public until 11:53 AM. It also explains the focus on United 93, about whose "crash" United did not tell employees until 10:15 AM.

Hypothesis: United originally told the AP that United 93 was the plane that landed in Cleveland. This was either a mistake or a plan by plotters using United as dupes to remove United 93 from the list of planes that would be "hijacked." This would explain the AP post having centered on United 93.

Hypothesis: United realized at some point subsequently that United 93 was nowhere near the Cleveland airport. It then heard Mayor White describe a plane with details unlike United 93. Relieved, United called AP and asked them to drop the post or to clarify the earlier conversation by saying the plane was Delta 1989.

This turn of events may seem a bit confusing, but the idea of the media and the airlines' employees feeling confused on 9/11 does not stretch the imagination.

Hypothesis: The AP probably rushed the job and corrected the initial post only partially. They got the "Boeing 767 out of Boston" portion edited but left[83] the rest of the message as indicating that it was United 93. They also failed to update the message to include mention of the events at the World Trade Center, the Pentagon, and Shanksville.

It sounds as though someone spotted the error quickly, which would account for the link to be removed promptly.

Hypothesis: Another plane landed in Cleveland at 10:45 AM. It may have been United 175, who had the time to make it. Also, United had to put the plane somewhere away from its alleged crash at the World Trade Center.

Were There Any Passengers in Cleveland?

Newspaper reports[84] mention approximately 200 people in an airplane at the west end of the airport, close to the NASA building, in late morning. These people had gotten on a plane that has not been accounted for.

---

[83] http://goo.gl/i2QJEz
[84] http://goo.gl/5MKeFh

We know the number was an approximation with no apparent source.

The lack of source does not make the information inaccurate. It simply deprives researchers of a chance to determine how the number 200 came to be asserted.

It is, however, interesting to note that the total number[85] of alleged passengers on all alleged flights associated with the events of 9/11 is also approximately 200. Counting all crewmembers, passengers and alleged hijackers, the total number is 265.

Of course, if only United 93 and United 175 flew, it may make sense to discount the crewmembers of American 11 and American 77 (11 and 6, respectively, or 17 total). This would lower the number to 248. Cutting out the number of alleged hijackers, 19, brings the total number down to 229.

Two of the flights were unscheduled and did not fly (American 11 and 77). A check of the Bureau of Transportation Statistics records, as noted earlier, in original and in "amended" form, shows this to be the case.

---

[85] http://en.wikipedia.org/wiki/September_11_attacks

As noted, United 175 could conceivably have made it to Cleveland in time to be the plane to which Mayor White referred. There were also reports of a plane matching the description of United 93 landing in Akron. No other details have emerged about this flight.

I now have serious doubts that anyone flew on either United 175 or United 93. The evidence in favor of this claim is similar to the evidence regarding passengers for American 11 and 77: There are allegations of copies of alleged passenger lists, manifests, and boarding passes.

But how can one take these documents seriously if one believes, as I do, that neither American 11 nor American 77 flew that day nor were even scheduled for the reasons given above?

It has never been clear how the names of passengers came to the attention of the public. The FBI took the lead in investigating the "crashes" and would have logically asked the airlines for the flight manifests, which would state definitively who boarded the plane.

I do not think anyone has seen the true manifests, quite possibly because they do not exist. What some call manifests were little more than lists of passengers that parties to the Zacarias Moussaoui case stipulated to (that is to say, the supposedly adversarial parties agreed as a matter of expediting the trial, not because they necessarily believed the manifests to be authentic).

The FBI then likely composed lists and sent them to various media outlets. These are the lists most people who have followed this matter have seen.

Some of these names show up on the Social Security Death Index (SSDI). But it should be noted that there is no way to verify any particular name from the four alleged flights of 9/11 because the chain of evidence in the government in producing these names is unclear.

It should be noted that the FBI, which gathered the names, also controlled the autopsies of the "passengers." And the report of the autopsies is what is typically needed to obtain a death certificate and to place a name on the SSDI.

There are other problems with using the SSDI to verify the existence of names that appear on passenger lists, as the next chapter will clearly establish.

Dean T. Hartwell

THE SEARCH FOR PASSENGERS

Dean T. Hartwell

Why the SSDI Proves Nothing as to 9/11

I checked to see if the names of passengers are the names of people on the Social Security Death Index (SSDI), which boasts an 85 percent accuracy rate.

In *Rumors Fly, Truth Walks: How Lies Become Our History*, I located 59 names from the 9/11 passenger lists on the SSDI of a total of 246 alleged passengers from the four alleged flights: American 11 and 77 and United 93 and 175. This comes out to a little less than 24 percent of the total. What is the significance of this finding?

To answer that question, here are important guidelines to consider in judging the accuracy of the SSDI:

> *The Social Security Death Index consists of an online searchable database. It only includes the names of deceased individuals whose deaths were reported to Social Security. This index is a master index file of deaths reported to the Social Security Administration. It has been kept since 1962, when operations were computerized.*

The index includes about 50 percent of deceased persons from 1962 to 1971 and about 85 percent of the deceased persons from 1972 to 2005. It also includes a few deaths from 1937 to 1961. Current as of September 30, 2012.[86]

Eighty-five percent! So who does NOT make the list?

The SSDI does not include death records for everyone who has been issued a Social Security Number (card). Common reasons for exclusion include the following:

The death was not reported to the Social Security Administration (SSA).

The death occurred before the Death Master File was maintained in a computer database. About 98 percent of the deaths in this database occurred between 1962 and the present.

The person did not participate in the Social Security program.

---

[86] https://goo.gl/rbGEVD

[Author's Note: Non-U.S. citizens who do not work in the United States usually do not have Social Security Numbers.]

Survivor death benefits were (are) being paid to dependents or spouse.

A recent death may not be indexed yet.

Human error.[87]

Who receives survivor death benefits?

Certain family members may be eligible to receive monthly benefits, including the following:

—A widow or widower age 60 or older (age 50 or older if disabled);

—A widow or widower at any age who is caring for the deceased's child under age 16 or disabled;

—An unmarried child of the deceased who is: younger than age 18 (or up to age 19 if he or she is a full-time student in an elementary or

---

[87] http://helpdesk.rootsweb.com/ssdi/index.html#reasons

secondary school) or age 18 or older with a disability that began before age 22;

—A stepchild, grandchild, step grandchild, or adopted child under certain circumstances;

—Parents, age 62 or older, who were dependent on the deceased for at least half of their support; and

—A surviving divorced spouse, under certain circumstances."[88]

I re-reviewed the names on the United 93 passenger list and their background stories. I then categorized the names as well. Those with relatives who could still receive survivor benefits were listed as having QUALIFYING SURVIVORS.

There may have been "passengers" who had qualifying survivors in September 2001 but do not have them now. This is because their children may have reached the age of 18, their widows and widowers may have passed on, etc. How can the proper interpretation of the SSDI help us to understand the people whose names are on the passenger lists? Here is one example of how to interpret the facts.

---

[88] http://www.ssa.gov/planners/survivors/

One of those "passengers," Todd Beamer, appears on the list for United 93 and on the SSDI. However, the date of death shown is "June 10, 1997." Also, his middle initial on the SSDI is "E," and the Beamer associated with Flight 93 is said to have had the middle initial "M" for the name Morgan.[89]

What is the significance of these facts? Probably nothing.

Todd Morgan Beamer allegedly died on September 11, 2001, leaving behind a widow, Lisa, two young sons, aged three and one, and a daughter born after his death. With the likelihood of his widow and/or the children receiving survivor benefits, his Social Security number would still be in use, and, therefore, it should be no surprise he is not on the SSDI. Perhaps his name will appear in 2020 when his daughter (Morgan Beamer) turns 18.

In summary, the SSDI does little good to either prove or disprove the life or death of anyone on the passenger lists.

However, few families of passengers, whether listed on the SSDI or not, took the "9-11 Victims Compensation Fund"—a special fund that

---

[89] http://en.wikipedia.org/wiki/Todd_Beamer

families could collect by merely promising not to sue the airlines.[90]

We can only guess why anyone would refuse this money, thought to be in the hundreds of thousands of dollars for those who took it. It is just another indication that the story about the passengers does not pass the smell test.

Lists of names may well have been prepared ahead of time and finalized on the day of the event to minimize the chance of including people who could state that they did not take the flight. The names include real people, people who had already died and fictitious names. The pictures could be composites so that no one could recognize themselves.

Without a Hijacking, Who Were the "Hijackers"?

The official theory tells us that Osama bin Laden trained members of al-Qaeda and sent them to the United States for flight training, but it fails to show proof that these members were on the planes. A videotape has emerged of Mohammed Atta and Abdulaziz Al-Omari at the Portland, Maine, airport, but the video shows two separate times. Another videotape

---

[90] http://www.wingtv.net/thornarticles/911passengerlist.html

purportedly shows other hijackers at the Dulles Airport in Washington, DC, but it gives no date or time.

According to the *9/11 Commission Report*, Atta left his baggage behind at Boston's Logan airport with incriminating evidence, including the names of all hijackers and his own will. If Atta intended to fly a plane to his death, he could not possibly have expected his will to remain intact after the crash. It is possible that he could have arranged for his bags to miss his flight (and completely fool the airline staff).

However, Atta himself had reportedly told his fellow hijackers to "check all of your items— your bag, your clothes, knives, your will, your IDs, your passport, your papers. . . . Make sure that nobody is following you."[91]

Between the two possibilities of Atta leaving an easy trail of evidence to help investigators solve the crime or someone using his name to frame him and mislead investigators, the latter appears more likely. The first scenario seems too simple to be true, like a murderer publicly announcing his next victim.

---

[91] http://goo.gl/zFRgLH

The FBI posted the names and other identifying information such as birthdays, place of birth, and home city about the 19 hijackers promptly after 9/11. When confronted with evidence that some of the hijackers listed were actually alive, the FBI Director Robert Mueller at first admitted that there was "no legal proof to the identities of the suicidal hijackers"[92] and then reverted back to his original position that the FBI had it right all along.

In fact, mainstream media sources have revealed that people with the same names and other identifying information of hijackers were alive after 9/11. Following is a list of the names of the alleged hijackers by flight and who allegedly lived past 9/11:

American Airlines Flight 11

- Waleed al-Shehri—LIVED
- Wail al-Shehri—LIVED
- Abdulaziz al-Omari—LIVED
- Mohammed Atta
- Satam M.A. Al Suqami

---

[92] http://goo.gl/ZPwG7s

American Airlines Flight 77

- Salem al-Hazmi—LIVED
- Khamid Almihdhar
- Majed Moqed
- Nawaf Alhazmi
- Hani Hanjour

United Airlines Flight 93

- Ahmed al-Nami—LIVED
- Saeed al-Ghamdi—LIVED
- Ahmed Ibrahim A. Al Haznawi
- Ziad Samir Jarrah

United Airlines Flight 175

- Mohand al-Shehri—LIVED
- Marwan Al-Shehhi
- Fayez Rashid Ahmed Hassan Al Qadi Banihammad
- Ahmed Alghamdi
- Hamza Alghamdi[93]

If these 19 men truly intended to hijack planes and crash them into buildings, they would probably use their real names since they might not fear capture and would want others to remember them. But the official theory ignores this problem. Their only reasonable remedy to

---

[93] http://www.whatreallyhappened.com/hijackers.html

the problem of the living people identified in error as participants would be to acknowledge negligence.

Barring a stunning coincidence that several sets of people from the same city have the same name, birthplace, and birthday, the FBI listed a number of names of people not connected to the attacks.

To clear up this discrepancy and dispel rumors of alleged FBI involvement (at least after the fact), the Bureau should correct its list of suspects and provide an explanation as to its initial mistake. Its failure to do so raises doubts about the true identities of the hijackers and hints at a cover-up of the true participants.

The FBI has also claimed that it has identified at least 10 of the hijackers by matching their remains to known DNA samples. Where did the samples come from?

Ellen Barakove, a spokeswoman for the New York Medical Examiner's office, said the FBI took the samples from "locations such as the scene of the crashes, a hotel, or other places where the hijackers stayed" the night before.[94]

---

[94] http://goo.gl/qnn1NX

But the same article fails to mention what the samples were matched to!

There Are No Authentic Manifests

The late researcher Jack White quotes[95] expert pilot John Lear, who shared information that calls into question what constitutes an authentic manifest. He says that passenger flights have, as required by the Federal Aviation Administration, what is called "The Envelope."

The Envelope contains "the final passenger manifest, the destination, the amount of fuel on board, the names of the pilot and flight attendants, etc. and the time the DOOR OF THE AIRCRAFT WAS CLOSED." According to Lear, the chief pilot signs the document.

White continues his recitation of Lear's words:[96]

> *The passenger manifest (a printout of pre-ticketed passengers) may be augmented by the chief flight attendant if passengers do not show up, or late arrivals are added. The manifest in THE ENVELOPE*

---

[95] https://goo.gl/3ZWBpL
[96] ibid

would include the names of hijackers, if pre-ticketed, or their written in aliases if added at the last moment by hand. In any event, every person on board would be accounted for.

I have never seen or heard of <u>THE official manifest</u> that the airline has with each flight. A true investigation would subpoena the airlines for this document to identify who actually boarded the plane.

Better yet, we should ask if there really are official airline manifests. How do people learn that loved ones have died on plane crashes? Someone contacts them with this information. The airline would make sense as they should be the first to know about an accident. How would they know whom to call and what number to call?

There is an even more compelling issue staring right at us: no one witnesses anyone die in any of the supposed plane crashes.

Everything we have learned has been provided by people who did not see and thus could not corroborate this tragedy.

To put this salient fact into perspective, I recall a train crash that took place some years ago just outside the building where I worked. I did not witness this tragedy but heard directly from some people who did right away as I arrived that day.

I had also seen several helicopters in the air as I was driving to work, a sure sign of some type of emergency. The radio stations all reported a train accident in the part of the City where I worked.

It wasn't just allegations of fatalities. I would hear the names of two people with whom I knew personally as among the fatalities reported by my employer and by the local media. I never saw these acquaintances again and have never doubted their passing.

The events of 9/11 were local to nothing. People claim to have seen airplanes striking the World Trade Center and the Pentagon but no one could ever positively identify the specific flights of American 11, United 175 and American 77. Conveniently (?) these "planes" did not yield identifiable pieces. And the DNA supposedly found at the "crash scenes" did not have names or other identification on them.

We have relied upon people far away from us to make the much-needed identifications of these passengers and planes. Would a manifest really convince us of something too convenient to believe to begin with?

The same problem hold true with the so-called relatives:

Allegations of Relatives Prove Nothing

The passengers have not spoken and the plotters will not speak. That leaves the relatives as the only group of people who may know what happened.

Hypothesis I: *The relatives received no notice before receiving phone calls from the passengers.*

If that is the case, then the relatives were left out of the plan and thus had no leverage as to the fate of the passengers. Most likely, the passengers are dead.

Hypothesis II: *The relatives received notice about the calls before receiving them.*

If that is the case, then the relatives may have been (coerced?) into a deal: for their silence, they would receive assurances that the passengers would not be harmed.

MOST LIKELY SCENARIO: Unknown. Only the relatives can tell us anything about this topic. Or perhaps the relatives are not being forthright.

The reaction of the relatives of the passengers to the news of the plane crashes can best be described as perplexing. None of the passengers' relatives are reported to have arrived at either destination airport, as is common when plane crashes take place. In an accident that took place in Taipei involving a plane that was destined for Los Angeles, the airport set up a Counseling Center[97] for the relatives of the victims.

Theories about the "Passengers"

Without cooperation from the alleged relatives, we cannot ascertain the identities or even the true number of passengers. The main problems of reaching this conclusion revolve around the fact that there is no way to prove, or falsify, the most plausible hypotheses, while other hypotheses are untenable.

Hypothesis 1: The passengers and relatives are genuine (real people and real names used). The passengers boarded Flights 175

---

[97] http://news.bbc.co.uk/2/hi/americas/1001087.stm

and 93 under their true names and went to Cleveland.[98] The relatives sincerely believe them to be dead.

Problem: They most certainly did not die at the alleged crash scenes. So the authorities have lied to the families, and yet we are expected to believe that none of them have figured this out?

Hypothesis 2: The passengers and relatives are genuine. The passengers boarded Flights 175 and 93 under their true names and went to Cleveland or another location. The relatives are told the passengers died in Cleveland.

Problem: It would not take long for any of the family members to realize that the plotters would be responsible for their relatives' deaths. That they would keep quiet about such an outrage is laughable.

Hypothesis 3: The passengers and relatives are genuine but are also in on the plot. The passengers boarded Flights 175 and 93 under their true names and went to Cleveland or another location. The relatives strike a deal with the plotters—silence in exchange for the

---

[98] Or somewhere nearby. As mentioned, I cannot verify that either United 93 or United 175 landed in Cleveland. The ACARS data suggests that both landed in that vicinity.

promise that the relatives are somewhere, unharmed.

Problem: It is hard to believe that people would accept the absence of their relatives unquestioningly, even for money. Also, how do we prove a deal was made or even that there is a connection between the relatives and the plotters? If money were involved, how would it be traced?

Hypothesis 4: The passengers used false names and/or false photographs that were later used to "identify" them. The relatives are genuinely related and could use false identities themselves. The passengers boarded Flights 175 and 93 under false names and went to Cleveland or another location. The relatives strike the same deal as in Hypothesis 3.

Problems: 1) the same disbelief as to why the relatives would go along with the plan; 2) the same questions as to proof, which are made more complex because of the use of false identities; and the same issues over money linger as well.

But the ease with which the passengers could be brought back into society increases as the identities make it harder for researchers to make connections. Fake pictures (see the "vicsim" pictures on sites like Let's Roll Forums[99] and September Clues[100]) provide even more cover. The issue of proof involves the ability of researchers to find out if the identities of passengers were identities of people who had any history before 9/11.

Hypothesis 5: (Variation of Hypothesis 4) The passengers could have all been agents using fake names and fake pictures. They could have gone to Cleveland or another location and then checked in with a new identity after 9/11. But how can this agency be proven and why waste so many agents on these flights?

I refused to give up. On a personal note, my parents are both computer programmers. One of the first words I learned as a child was "debug," or clear errors out of a program. I would watch them make guess after guess as to what was keeping their program from succeeding until they found the correct one. It was very much like the idea of generating and testing hypotheses until one worked.

So I took another look at pictures on Let's Roll Forums and September Clues. I reread an article on the latter as to how a picture of one

---

[99] http://letsrollforums.com/
[100] http://www.septemberclues.info/

alleged victim, Honor Elizabeth Wainio, could be used to make several pictures of her. With her and with other alleged passengers, there are different pictures with the same lighting and facial expression, which would be highly unlikely of real people.

If even one picture and corresponding identity were faked, I reasoned, any or all of the others could be faked as well. So I came up with a new hypothesis based on Hypothesis #5 in narration form:

Early on the morning of September 11, 2001, approximately 200 intelligence agents showed up, some of them at Boston Airport and others at Newark Airport.

Upon orders from a connection to the plot, they take their false identities and board Flight 175 (Boston) and Flight 93 (Newark). In both cases, separate groups of agents arrive late and fill the plane with more passengers than are officially indicated. The high number of people on board (and their visibility) is designed to confuse the public into believing that neither plane could be United 93 or United 175 (which officially had 33 and 56 passengers, respectively).

Photographs and false identities have already been created for all of the alleged passengers.

Some names of real people, like Barbara Olson, are used as well to create the impression that only real names were used. These photographs are kept handy until it was time to release some of them to the media.

The two flights clear the area and head toward Cleveland, where they land after the orders are given by the FAA for all airplanes to land as soon as possible. Flight plans are altered and images on screens are tampered with to create the impression that Flight 175 came back east and went to New York and that Flight 93 came back east and went to Pennsylvania. Similar trickery is employed for the fake flights of 11 and 77.

At least one set of agents lands in Cleveland and, after a short time of detention on their planes, they head quietly to the NASA building. There some of the plotters de-brief the agents as to what has happened on the East Coast.

The plotters release the names of some of the passengers over the next few days and some of the "relatives" get clearance from the plotters to speak to the media. They create a narration of hijacked passengers who died as part of what would eventually become known as the "War on Terror" against Islamic fundamentalists. The "relatives" are so loyal to the official theory that one may reasonably wonder if they are themselves agents, perhaps even the same ones!

The agents wait in Cleveland for further instructions. During this time, some of the agents work with the plotters to knock down stories in the media, such as the one in which the Associated Press quoted United Airlines as saying that United 93 landed in Cleveland.

The Problem of Non-Falsifiability

The problem with making determinations about people boarding either United 93 or United 175 is that no one can prove it. To assert that any one person did or did not fly is simply non-falsifiable.

Passenger lists or even manifests could be faked, for example.

People could have boarded under false names.

Passengers could have included those not listed in the SSDI, which is, as mentioned above, not a reliable source of information if it cannot be established that the person in question ever lived.

There is one more idea about the true role of "passengers" to consider upon reviewing three people known to have lived before 9/11 and their stories.

CASE STUDIES OF THREE "PASSENGERS"

Dean T. Hartwell

CASE STUDY PASSENGER TIMELINE

Here is the chronology of the media discussion of two of the "passengers" who received the most attention, Barbara Olson and Todd Beamer:

9/11/01 – Late in the day, CNN posted a story that Ted Olson said that his wife, Barbara, had called him from the plane (American 77)[101]

9/13 – Larry Ellison, CEO of Oracle, Todd Beamer's employer, sends a memo to his employees praising Beamer's bravery on United 93.[102]

9/14 – Lisa Beamer, wife of Todd, learns for first time that Todd made a phone call from United 93 to a GTE/Verizon operator who gave the call to her supervisor, Lisa Jefferson, contacts Beamer by letter telling her she is available to talk to her.[103] Lisa Beamer receives "synopsis" of the conversation

---

[101] http://goo.gl/7GU4Y

[102] http://goo.gl/GK0DVs

[103] Jefferson, Lisa and Felicia Middlebrooks. *Called: "Hello, My Name is Mrs. Jefferson. I Understand Your Plane is Being Hijacked."*; Northfield Publishing; 2006; 78

between Todd Beamer and Lisa Jefferson this evening.[104]

9/16 – The phrase "Let's Roll" is quoted in print for the first time by Jim McKinnon of the Pittsburgh Post-Gazette.[105]

---

[104] Davidsson, 189
[105] http://goo.gl/4DcFvU

THE STORY OF 11X

I received an email not long ago from a man who claimed he knew personally a specific person said to be a passenger on Flight 11. He alluded to a source who claimed that he had overheard the passenger, whom I will call "11X," calling a taxi on the morning of September 11, 2001 and then had seen board with luggage a taxi shortly thereafter. He claims neither he nor anyone else who knew him has seen 11X again.

I will assume the good faith of the claims of the man who emailed me. He gave me his name and I looked him up on public sources. Let's say that 11X was in fact a real person who indicated to others he would take a flight from Boston to Los Angeles on that morning and that 11X's name ended up on a passenger list.

How does this stipulation fit in with the facts established about the flight?

11X shows up at Boston's Logan Airport. He goes to one of the two gates alleged for Flight 11's departure, Gate 26 or Gate 32. He boards the plane he believes is Flight 11.

A link on Let's Roll Forums (discussed in detail later) regarding flight attendant phone calls, gives evidence that Flight 11 was really a simulation. It further cites early reports about Flight 11 sitting on the ground at the airport several minutes after it allegedly took off.[106]

Upon realizing that Flight 11 was not going to fly, 11X most likely would have looked for another flight to go to Los Angeles. This would put him at Gate 19.

He had time to get from either Gate 32 or Gate 26 to go to Gate 19. In the first edition of *Planes without Passengers: The Faked Hijackings of 9/11*, I suggested that he (and other passengers) could have been "taxied" by a plane to Gate 19. Some say that such a plane would have been noticed. Maybe so. If it were noticed, there is no telling if anyone reporting it would have been believed or paid much attention to.

Furthermore, the plane would have gone around a corner, possibly losing the interest of onlookers. With a little effort, passengers could make the distance on foot, anyway.

---

[106] http://goo.gl/2J0X0B

In any case, 11X now boards United 175.

If he had had an American Flight 11 ticket, he could have quickly gone to the United Airlines booth and exchanged tickets for the 175 flight. And who is to say what ticket 11X held? With no direct information on this matter, it is possible to theorize that he was instructed to go to United 175 all along.

United 175 takes off (late, according to some sources). This flight was flying WEST over Western Pennsylvania several minutes AFTER its supposed crash into World Trade Center Two.

An unidentified plane (by flight number) may have landed in Cleveland sometime later, matching the description of the plane for United 175.

IF the plane was indeed United 175, this could place 11X at Cleveland's Hopkins Airport.

Newspaper articles cite a plane with 200 passengers sitting at the west end of the airport,[107] close to a building managed by

---

[107] http://goo.gl/PYsuoq

NASA, which had been evacuated about 9:45 AM.[108]

Here is where I erred previously. The newspapers never give a source of anyone who claimed to have seen 200 passengers. Perhaps there was a group of people walking toward the NASA building, but I cannot find a source to better my understanding of the truth or falsity of this claim.

We have only the word of my source that 11X has not been seen or heard from by his family or friends since September 11, 2001. His execution or his (perhaps forced) decision to hide both explain his absence.

Those who insist he was murdered could point to his character or his ties to the community but neither prove the point. If he went into hiding (as an agent, for example), there may be circumstantial evidence of participation but no proof.

Let's try our luck with a passenger from another non-flight.

---

[108] http://goo.gl/euZd9B

WHAT HAPPENED TO BARBARA OLSON?

With no facts on any flight, passengers, or phone calls, it is obvious the whole story of American Airlines 77 is fiction. The best start for analysis is with the alleged passengers.

The most well-known person allegedly on the plane was Barbara Olson. Theories range as to her whereabouts. Some say she was killed off by the plotters, while others say she went away, perhaps to come back later with a new identity.

According to Ted Olson in an interview with Larry King days after the "crash," Barbara had originally planned to fly from Virginia to Los Angeles on Monday, September 10th. She changed her mind and decided to take the flight on September 11th so that she could spend time with Ted as his birthday was that day.[109]

In the same interview, Ted relates that Barbara stayed overnight with him and awoke with him Tuesday morning. He says that he went to work "very early in the morning, before 6" and that she "left shortly after that to go to the airport." Again in the same interview, Ted tells

---

of a brief conversation the two of them had, in which he apparently thought she was boarding or about to board a plane.

We know that Ted Olson was untruthful about receiving phone calls from Barbara while she was aboard the airplane. Here he makes a number of statements in which the only person likely to be able to confirm them is "dead."

Do we know for sure that Barbara stayed over the night of the 10th? Has anyone found the vehicle by which she got to the airport, or stated that they saw her on it?

What happened to Barbara Olson? Here are some hypotheses based on facts that will help us arrive at the most likely answer to the question of what happened to her.

Hypothesis I: Olson was killed

Reasonable Doubts: Olson could have been an asset to the plotters alive. As a political commentator, she knew the media well and could have advised them as to where to "place" stories supporting the official theory.

Hypothesis II: Olson lived

Reasonable Doubts: If a publicly well-known "passenger" like Olson ever showed up alive, the official story would collapse. Keeping her alive would be a great risk to the plotters.

WHAT HAPPENED TO TODD BEAMER?

No alleged passenger achieved more fame than Todd Beamer. According to the legend spread through the media, Beamer, confronted by terrorists on United 93, shouted the battle cry "Let's Roll!" He inspired other passengers to fight back and forced the terrorists to crash the plane in a field in Shanksville, Pennsylvania.

According to the official story...

Beamer worked for Oracle Corporation selling systems applications and software.[110] Shortly before September 11, 2001, Beamer took a trip to Italy with his wife, Lisa, as a reward from Oracle for his excellence in salesmanship.

Like Barbara Olson, Todd Beamer apparently had the choice of taking a Monday, September

---

[110] http://en.wikipedia.org/wiki/Todd_Beamer#cite_note-AmNatBiography-3

10th flight to get to his destination (San Francisco) or taking the Tuesday flight. A Pittsburgh Post-Gazette article in October 2001 noted that Beamer chose to stay at home on the 10th to be with his family.[111]

Like Ted Olson, Lisa Beamer apparently did not see her spouse leave the house that day or at least does not say in what vehicle he may have left.[112] She acknowledges she knew little about the details of his itineraries and in fact thought at first he took a flight on Continental Airlines.[113]

These details may well be insignificant, but they also leave room open for legends to be written.

Beamer made his alleged shout "Let's Roll" into a telephone that Verizon operator Lisa Jefferson would later say she heard. For several days after this event, Jefferson supposedly was the only person to know of

---

[111] http://old.post-gazette.com/headlines/20011028flt93beamerbiop8.asp
[112] Beamer, Lisa and Ken Abraham. *Let's Roll! Ordinary People, Extraordinary Courage*; Alive Communications; Colorado Springs; 2002; 2.
[113] Ibid, 5.

Beamer's call and the story of a passenger uprising against hijackers.

However, Oracle CEO Larry Ellison sent out a memo to his employees long before the call became public. His memo read:

> We know Todd Beamer is dead. We believe he died when he and other passengers aboard Flight 93 tried to recover the hijacked airplane from the terrorists.... Considering the devastation wrought by the other aircraft, it is unquestionable that Todd's brave actions, and [those] of his fellow passengers, saved countless lives on the ground.[114]

Lisa Beamer would later write in her book about Todd, *Let's Roll!: Ordinary People, Extraordinary Courage*:

> How did Larry know that? The FBI hadn't made any announcement to that effect. Todd's name had not shown up in any reports indicating

---

that he might have been involved in some way.[115]

Could Ellison have known about Beamer's story through Oracle's connections to the CIA? Evidence shows that the company got its start as a CIA-run project involving some of the people who would later become its leaders.[116]

Strangely, Jefferson said later in her own book, *Called: Hello, My Name Is Mrs. Jefferson. I Understand Your Plane Is Being Hijacked. 9:45 Am, Flight 93, September 11, 2001*, that she offered to put Beamer through to his wife. Todd inexplicably refused, instead spending the last few minutes of his life on the phone with a stranger!

Consensus 9/11, a group of experts on the facets of the events of 9/11, lists several other reasons to doubt the validity of the alleged call from Todd Beamer to Lisa Jefferson, such as the fact Jefferson had never before heard Beamer's voice, Jefferson failed to record the

[115] Beamer and Abraham, 195.

[116] http://www.sfgate.com/bayarea/article/Oracle-s-coziness-with-government-goes-back-to-2820370.php

call, and the last call went on for 65 minutes, long after the "crash"![117]

But perhaps the most intriguing issue is that the FBI did not mention Beamer's famous battle cry "Let's Roll" in the summary of their interview with Jefferson on September 11, 2001.[118] This phrase did not go public until an article written by Jim McKinnon of the Pittsburgh Post-Gazette five days later. McKinnon claims that Lisa Beamer told him that Todd had likely used the phrase.[119] The phrase that just happened to become the national battle cry against the "terrorists."

So where was Todd Beamer on that day?

As with Olson, we have only a spouse's claim of the "passenger" staying overnight before a postponed trip. We have no way to verify how he got to the airport. We can also state without reservation that any call he may have made was not about real hijackers or a real crash.

Todd Beamer likely took the approach I have outlined above for Barbara Olson. He never boarded any plane. Someone from Oracle

---

[117] http://www.consensus911.org/point-pc-1/
[118] http://goo.gl/vY6KeV (Intelwire.com)
[119] http://goo.gl/4DcFvU

could have provided personal information about Beamer to whoever made the call.

The caller could have given enough personal information to convince Jefferson and Lisa Beamer that Todd indeed made the call. With his company's CIA connections, he could easily have assumed a new identity after the "crash."

Writing in her book *Called*, Jefferson says she believes that she spoke with Todd Beamer and believes that he was on a hijacked airplane. But Jefferson may have unwittingly provided a hint of doubt. She writes in her introduction in reference to the events of September 11, 2001:

> We can live our days trying to make sense of the senseless, or we can trust God...and trust sometimes requires unanswered questions.[120]

Such a belief, especially put forth by the powers in our society who used Jefferson's story to sell the official story, stymies reasonable inquiry.

---

[120] Jefferson, Lisa and Felicia Middlebrooks. 17.

Is Lisa Jefferson letting questions go unanswered or is she unwilling to reveal answers to those questions?

Dean T. Hartwell

THE SEARCH FOR PHONE CALLS

Dean T. Hartwell

David Ray Griffin and AK Dewdney

David Ray Griffin[121] explains the utter lack of consistency in the official explanations of phone calls on the planes associated with 9/11. He does an excellent job of explaining how the FBI at first remained silent (in 2001) as to what phones were used on the planes.

He then shows the chronology of A.K. Dewdney's report (which made it clear that cell phone calls were then only reasonably possible at altitudes of less than 2,000 feet) to that of the subsequent FBI report for the 2006 Zacarias Moussaoui trial, which changed many of the calls from cell to air phone.[122]

From Griffin's analysis of the work of researchers like Dewdney, we can easily surmise that the official story on the number of cell phones (now given by the FBI as mostly air phones) changed drastically after it became known publicly the difficulty in getting cell phones to work at typical airplane altitudes.

---

[121] http://goo.gl/oacM8V
[122] ibid

Here is a look at each flight and alleged calls:

American 11

Timeline including phone calls

7:40 AM—Boarding

7:59 AM—Take off

8:13 AM—The pilots' last radio communication is made from the pilots to ground control: "twenty right American eleven."[123]

8:15 AM—Boston Air Traffic Control begins unsuccessful attempts to contact the pilots after the plane fails to respond to an order to climb.[124]

8:20 AM—American 11 stops transmitting its transponder signal and veers northward and departs dramatically from the westward heading of its planned route. The controllers conclude that the plane has probably been hijacked.[125]

8:21-8:46—Amy (Madeline) Sweeney, one of the flight attendants, calls Michael Woodward from airline's field services.[126] (Cell)

---

[123] http://goo.gl/ZrGgfP
[124] http://goo.gl/2Gsu5o
[125] http://911research.wtc7.net/planes/attack/flight11.html#ref4
[126] http://goo.gl/IdmRv1

8:21-8:46—Betty Ong, another flight attendant, calls Vanessa Minter at the airline's reservations.[127] (Air)

8:24 AM—The following transmission is reportedly received from Flight 11:

> *We have some planes. Just stay quiet and you'll be okay ... we are returning to the airport.*
>
> *...Nobody move. Everything will be okay. If you try to make any moves, you'll endanger yourself and the airplane. Just stay quiet.*
>
> *Nobody move please we are going back to the airport ... don't try to make any stupid moves.*[128]

8:28 AM—controllers reportedly watch the plane make a 100-degree turn toward the south.[129]

8:46 AM—The plane crashes into the World Trade Center (north building), killing everyone on board.

---

[127] Ibid
[128] http://goo.gl/sA0zlb
[129] http://goo.gl/iuCaEz

The Callers and Calls

The phone calls from two of the crewmembers of "flight" American 11 have been determined to have likely been calls made from the ground during a simulation of a hijacking.[130]

A researcher, known as "loopDloop," wrote an article in July 2012 called "Fog, Fiction and the Flight 11 Phone Calls" that appeared on the *Let's Roll Forums* website. The article reveals the presence of two recordings of the same phone call from flight attendant Betty Ong.

One recording sounds as though it covers up discussion the public was not supposed to hear. The author identifies evidence destruction.

Furthermore, the author points out that Ong does not identify where she is sitting because that would give away that she was using an air phone, which flight attendants are forbidden to use.

It becomes clear through the research that Ong was talking on a headset to operators about a fictitious hijacking.

---

[130] http://goo.gl/2J0X0B

Fellow flight attendant Amy Sweeney also made a call. Hers allegedly went to American Airlines Flight Service at Boston Logan Airport and transcripts apparently show that she identified where hijackers were.[131]

Interestingly, this use of a phone to transmit false messages could also easily explain the "voices from the cockpit" for this flight and the other three.

Evidence of phone calls on "Flight 11" suggests that the two flight attendants were taking part in a simulation and that their words were later used as "evidence" of a hijacking on the plane.

Ong's use of the term "Flight 12" and her statement "We're on Flight 11 *right now*"[132] suggest a conscious effort to use the wrong flight number. The idea that she used the "mistake" to signal something to listeners cannot be ruled out.

Listen to Ong's tone of voice in this YouTube clip and determine for yourself if she sounds like she is witnessing a hijacking.[133] It sounds

---

[131] http://goo.gl/gWEoMS
[132] http://goo.gl/jJUKPO
[133] https://goo.gl/d0GpQU

too quiet in the background and she sounds too calm.

This phone call served as a turning point for me. In considering these observations, I no longer envisioned planes or passengers at all.

I began to instead form a new picture in my mind: Betty Ong is sitting at a table reading from a script about a hijacking scenario. She reluctantly picks up the air phone, which has been removed from Flight 11's plane, and makes this call. In hearing the voices of people from Reservations, she wonders whether they are in on the simulation.

There are approximately twenty recorded minutes of Ong's conversation unreleased to the public. But hearing the four minute recording and picturing her frustration with the role she was asked to play casts a bright light pointing to the truth about the "calls" on other flights.

American 77

Timeline with Phone Calls

7:50 AM—Boarding

8:20 AM—Take-off

8:46 AM—Flight 77 veers severely off course.

8:50 AM—The last radio communication was made from the pilots and air traffic control.

8:55 AM—The plane begins to turn south.

8:56 AM—The jet's transponder is shut off.[134] The pilots' last transmission is "ah direct FALMOUTH American seventy seven thanks."

9:00 AM—The plane begins to head east. Shortly thereafter it begins to descend from its altitude of 35,000 feet. The autopilot is engaged and disengaged multiple times.

9:12 AM—Flight attendant Renee May calls her mother.[135]

9:12-9:26 AM—Barbara Olson allegedly makes calls to husband Ted Olson during this period of time.[136]

---

[134] http://goo.gl/9IrPS
[135] http://goo.gl/IdmRv1
[136] Ibid

9:29 AM—The plane is now 35 miles west of the Pentagon, flying at 7,000 feet.

9:34 AM—The plane is now about 3.5 miles west-southwest of the Pentagon and starts a 330-degree descending right turn, bringing it to an altitude of about 2,000 feet four miles southwest of the Pentagon.[137]

9:37 AM—The plane crashes into the west side of the Pentagon at 9:37 AM, killing everyone on board and 125 people who were in the building.[138]

Flight attendant Renee May allegedly used a cell phone to make a call to her mother.[139]

A study by GlobalResearch.ca points out that carrier AT&T records do not show proof of alleged passenger Barbara Olson making a call to her husband Ted Olson, the then-Solicitor General, though the government "routinely" keeps such records.[140]

Moreover, the FBI records reveal that one call was made during the time of American 77 to

---

[137] Ibid.
[138] http://en.wikipedia.org/wiki/American_Airlines_Flight_77
[139] http://goo.gl/Mtmwvl
[140] http://goo.gl/8fuJaU

the Justice Department (where Olson's husband Ted worked as the Solicitor General) but that the call was "unconnected."[141]

The calls, from Olson, and from other passengers, did not come from American 77 and were a part of a propaganda campaign to convince the public of the claims that Olson supposedly made—that there were terrorists with box cutters who hijacked and crashed the flight.

Seen through the light provided by my thoughts about Flight 11, the plotters used another flight attendant, May, to make a personal call from the ground. The official story needed the emotional tug of someone calling their mother.

Where was Barbara Olson? I do not "see" her in the simulation room with May. The evidence of her calling or attempting to call her husband is rather shallow.

The plotters needed her account of box cutters as no other caller was to say anything about that. With Barbara probably objecting to making a call to her husband, another person likely filled in and tried without success to reach Ted.

---

[141] https://goo.gl/R659th

United 93

Timeline with Phone Calls

8:00 AM—Forty-four people, including seven crew members, board United 93.[142]

8:28 AM—The flight took off from Newark Airport with San Francisco as its destination (Source: Bureau of Transportation Statistics).[143]

8:42 AM—The flight took off from Newark Airport with San Francisco as its destination (according to mainstream sources).[144]

9:16 AM—The FAA informs North American Aerospace Defense Command (NORAD) that the flight may have been hijacked.

9:27 AM—Several communications with air traffic controllers later indicate that Flight 93 is hijacked at around this time.[145]

9:30 AM—The transponder signal ceases. At about this time, the plane apparently reverses direction and begins flying toward the capital.[146]

---

[142] http://en.wikipedia.org/wiki/United_Airlines_Flight_93
[143] https://goo.gl/Vp7S45
[144] Ibid.
[145] http://www.cnn.com/2001/US/09/16/inv.hijack.warning/
[146] http://911research.wtc7.net/planes/attack/flight93.html

9:30 AM—Thomas Burnett, Jr. calls residence.[147]

9:36 AM—Sandra Bradshaw, flight attendant, calls United Airlines.

9:36—Mark Bingham calls his mother.

9:37 AM—Jeremy Glick makes call.

9:37 AM—Thomas Burnett, Jr. calls residence.

9:39-9:43—Lauren Grandcolas makes several calls during this time period.

9:41 AM—Mark Bingham calls his mother a second time.

9:42 AM—Joseph DeLuca makes call.

9:43 AM—Todd Beamer calls GTE operator.

9:43 AM—Joseph DeLuca makes second call.

9:44 AM—Thomas Burnett, Jr. calls residence third time.

9:46 AM—Linda Gronlund calls.

9:47 AM—CeeCee Lyles, flight attendant, calls her residence.

9:49 AM—Marion Britton makes phone call.

---

[147] https://goo.gl/qcfZwv - all calls from alleged United 93 passengers are taken from this source.

9:49 AM—Sandra Bradshaw, flight attendant, calls residence.

9:52 AM—Sandra Bradshaw, flight attendant, calls residence again.

9:53 AM—Honor Elizabeth Wainio calls her parents.

9:58 AM—Edward Felt makes phone call.

9:58 AM—CeeCee Lyles, flight attendant, again calls her residence.

10:03 AM—The plane crashes in a field in Shanksville, Pennsylvania, killing everyone on board.[148]

The Callers and the Calls

Following is a list of the passengers who allegedly made calls during the flight United 93. An asterisk is placed next to the name of the caller who was reported originally to have made a cell call and later said by the FBI to have used an air phone.[149]

- Todd Beamer
- Mark Bingham
- Sandy Bradshaw*

---

[148] http://en.wikipedia.org/wiki/United_Airlines_Flight_93
[149] http://goo.gl/oacM8V

- Marion Britton*
- Thomas Burnett*
- Joseph DeLuca
- Edward Felt
- Jeremy Glick*
- Lauren Grandcolas
- Linda Grunland
- CeeCee Lyles
- Honor Wainio*[150]

Why on earth was there any doubt as to what types of phones were used?

There are other issues worth pondering: according to the information provided by the government at the aforementioned Moussaoui trial:

(1) One call allegedly went past the time of the Shanksville "crash," Todd Beamer's last call on United 93.

(2) No records of calls are sourced to the companies that provided them. This fact calls into question the authenticity of the calls.

(3) Lisa Jefferson, who reportedly took Beamer's call, failed to mention the phrase

---

[150] http://goo.gl/2TCyvF

"Let's roll" in an interview with the Pittsburgh Post-Gazette, which introduced the heroics of Beamer and others on the flight. She also had never before heard Beamer's voice.

(4) In fact, the FBI delayed bringing out the story of "Let's roll" and the passengers "fighting back" and apparently only did so to stop the story of a flight shoot-down from gaining momentum.

I have trouble picturing a group of people simulating calls. Consider the following reported calls:

(1) A caller claiming to be passenger Mark Bingham said:

Caller: *"Mom? This is Mark Bingham. I want you to know that I love you. I'm on a flight from Newark to San Francisco and there are three guys who have taken over the plane and they say they have a bomb."*

Alice Hoagland: *"Who are these guys?*

Caller: *(after a pause) "You believe me, don't you?*

Alice: *"Yes, Mark. I believe you. But who are these guys?*

(2) Another supposed caller, Jeremy Glick, said, when asked if he and others were going to fight back against the hijackers, "I have my butter knife from breakfast." According to Dewdney:

This is strange because it implies that the caller had already finished breakfast, whereas meals are not normally served until the aircraft reaches cruising altitude, about the time that the alleged hijacking began.[151]

(3) A caller who said he was Todd Beamer[152] talked to a GTE/Verizon operator, Lisa Jefferson, for several minutes instead of preparing to take on the "terrorists" with other passengers. Beamer's behavior will be explored in fuller detail later.

I am not really picturing anything here. These comments and actions are illogical and out of context of an emergency. I am hearing the babble of poor imagination.

It sounds instead as though those who received the calls forgot their lines or the "roles"

---

[151] http://goo.gl/YyD1Gb
[152] http://physics911.net/cellphoneflight93/

that "relatives" or "loved ones" were supposed to play.

The calls were sold to the public to advance the "fact" that the hijackings and crashes happened. Of secondary importance are what phones were used and where the calls were made from.

These calls are part of what holds the official theory together. The plotters needed to make sure the **reports** of the calls got through and the information about hijackers was conveyed.

United 175

Timeline with Phone Calls

8:14 AM—Boston, Logan Airport. According to the official version of events, the flight takes off.

8:41 AM—A United 175 pilot reports that he has overheard a transmission (presumably from by-then-hijacked Flight 11):

> ya we figured we'd wait to go to you center ah we heard a suspicious transmission on our departure out of Boston ah with someone ah, ah sound like someone sound like someone keyed the mike and said ah everyone ah stay in your seats.

Shortly thereafter, the last radio communication is made from the pilots and air traffic control: "that's ah cut out ... did you copy that?"[153]

8:42 AM—United 175 veers off its planned course and begins flying south.[154]

8:43 AM—The FAA notifies NORAD that the flight had been hijacked.[155]

---

[153] http://nsarchive.gwu.edu/NSAEBB/NSAEBB196/doc03.pdf
[154] http://goo.gl/9lrPS
[155] http://911research.wtc7.net/planes/attack/flight175.html

8:46 AM—United 175 stops transmitting its transponder signal.[156]

8:52 AM—Peter Hanson begins a number of phone calls to his father.[157]

9:03 AM—United 175 strikes World Trade Center south tower, killing all aboard.[158]

The Callers and the Calls

There were relatively fewer alleged phone calls from United 175, but the calls, echoing the same story as the calls from United 93, were about hijackers.[159] [160]

Two passengers, Peter Hanson and Brian Sweeney, are said to have made calls during this "flight." Hanson made a call to his father and Sweeney attempted calls to his wife. The latter, not reaching her, left a message.[161]

There is no record of what times Sweeney made his calls. The media originally reported both callers as having used cell phones. The

---

[156] http://goo.gl/2Gsu5o
[157] http://911research.wtc7.net/planes/evidence/phonecalls.html
[158] http://en.wikipedia.org/wiki/United_Airlines_Flight_175
[159] https://goo.gl/ABg3fN
[160] https://goo.gl/v5csRq
[161] http://goo.gl/Mtmwvl

FBI contended five years later that they used air phones.

I don't picture a simulation here. The situation brought to the public's attention about this flight so little matches the intensity of Betty Ong's call or the story of United 93 that this flight may not have been much of a focus to the plotters.

Dean T. Hartwell

REVISED TIMELINE

Dean T. Hartwell

Source: www.911timeline.net unless otherwise noted. All times Eastern

7:40 AM—Boston, Logan Airport. Ninety-two people, including 11 crew members, are later said to board American 11, a Boeing 767-223ER.[162] The flight destination is Los Angeles.[163]

7:50 AM—Washington, Dulles Airport. Sixty-four people, including the five crew members, are later said to board American 77.

7:59 AM—American 11 allegedly takes off.

8:00 AM—Forty-four people, including seven crew members, allegedly board United 93, a Boeing 757-200 with registration number N591UA at gate A17 at Newark International Airport.[164]

8:13 AM—What is later said to be the pilots' last radio communication is made from the pilots to ground control: "twenty right American eleven."[165]

---

[162] http://en.wikipedia.org/wiki/American_Airlines_Flight_11
[163] http://goo.gl/1SejxY
[164] http://en.wikipedia.org/wiki/United_Airlines_Flight_93
[165] http://goo.gl/ZrGgfP

8:14 AM—At Boston's Logan Airport, 65 people, including nine crew members, allegedly board United 175.[166]

8:14 AM—United 175 allegedly takes off with Los Angeles as its destination.

8:15 AM—Boston Air Traffic Control begins unsuccessful attempts to contact the pilots of American 11 after the plane fails to respond to an order to climb.[167]

8:20 AM—American 11 stops transmitting its transponder signal and veers northward and departs dramatically from the westward heading of its planned route. The controllers conclude that the plane has probably been hijacked.[168]

8:20 AM—American 77, allegedly takes off with Los Angeles as its destination.[169]

8:21-8:46—Amy (Madeline) Sweeney, one of the Flight 11 attendants, calls Michael Woodward from airline's field services from a phone on the ground.[170]

---

[166] http://en.wikipedia.org/wiki/United_Airlines_Flight_175
[167] http://goo.gl/2Gsu5o
[168] http://911research.wtc7.net/planes/attack/flight11.html#ref4
[169] http://en.wikipedia.org/wiki/American_Airlines_Flight_77
[170] http://goo.gl/ldmRv1

8:21-8:46—Betty Ong, another Flight 11 attendant, calls Vanessa Minter at the airline's reservations with an air phone on the ground.[171]

8:23 AM—United 175 takes off from Boston Airport (Bureau of Transportation Statistics)

8:24 AM—The following transmission is reportedly received from Flight 11: *We have some planes. Just stay quiet and you'll be okay ... we are returning to the airport....Nobody move. Everything will be okay. If you try to make any moves, you'll endanger yourself and the airplane. Just stay quiet...Nobody move please we are going back to the airport ... don't try to make any stupid moves.*[172]

8:28 AM—controllers reportedly watch American 11 make a 100-degree turn toward the south.[173]

8:28 AM—United 93 takes off from Newark Airport with San Francisco as its destination (Source: Bureau of Transportation Statistics).[174]

---

[171] Ibid

[172] http://goo.gl/sA0zlb

[173] http://911research.wtc7.net/planes/attack/flight11.html#ref7

[174] https://goo.gl/Vp7S45

8:41 AM—A United 175 pilot reports that he has overheard a transmission (presumably from by-then-hijacked Flight 11):

> *ya we figured we'd wait to go to you center ah we heard a suspicious transmission on our departure out of Boston ah with someone ah, ah sound like someone sound like someone keyed the mike and said ah everyone ah stay in your seats.*

Shortly thereafter, the last radio communication is made from the pilots and air traffic control: "that's ah cut out ... did you copy that?"[175]

8:42 AM—United 175 veers off its planned course and begins flying south.[176]

8:42 AM—United 93 takes off from Newark Airport with San Francisco as its destination (according to mainstream media sources).[177]

8:43 AM—The FAA notifies NORAD that United 175 has been hijacked.[178]

---

[175] http://goo.gl/w7woZi
[176] http://goo.gl/9IrPS
[177] Ibid.
[178] http://911research.wtc7.net/planes/attack/flight175.html

8:43 AM—United 93 takes off from Newark Airport (MSNBC)[179]

8:46 AM—American 11 reportedly crashes into the World Trade Center (north building), killing everyone on board.

8:46 AM—Flight 77 allegedly veers severely off course.

8:46 AM—United 175 stops transmitting its transponder signal.[180]

8:50 AM—The last radio communication was reportedly made from the pilots of American 77 and air traffic control.

8:52 AM—Lee Hanson alleges he first received phone calls from his son, Peter, said to be a passenger on United 175.[181]

8:55 AM—American 77 begins to turn south.

8:56 AM—The jet's transponder is reportedly shut off.[182] The pilots' last transmission is "ah direct FALMOUTH American seventy seven thanks." No radio communications from the flight indicate distress.[183]

---

[179] http://goo.gl/x8r34P

[180] http://goo.gl/2Gsu5o

[181] http://911research.wtc7.net/planes/evidence/phonecalls.html

[182] http://goo.gl/9lrPS

[183] http://nsarchive.gwu.edu/NSAEBB/NSAEBB196/doc02.pdf

9:00 AM—American 77 allegedly begins to head east. Shortly thereafter it begins to descend from its altitude of 35,000 feet. The autopilot is engaged and disengaged multiple times.

9:03 AM—United 175 allegedly strikes World Trade Center south tower, killing all aboard.[184]

9:12 AM—Flight 77 attendant Renee May calls her mother from the ground.[185]

9:12-9:26 AM—Someone impersonating Barbara Olson attempts calls from the ground to Ted Olson during this period of time, alleging Barbara Olson is on American 77, a hijacked plane.[186]

9:16 AM—The FAA informs North American Aerospace Defense Command (NORAD) that United 93 may have been hijacked.

9:22 AM—United Airlines sends advisory to dispatchers that United 175 was involved in an "accident" in New York (History Commons)

9:23 AM—ACARS message receipt shows United 175 still flying near Pittsburgh, PA (Pilots for 9/11 Truth)

---

[184] http://en.wikipedia.org/wiki/United_Airlines_Flight_175
[185] http://goo.gl/ldmRv1
[186] Ibid

9:27 AM—Several communications with air traffic controllers later opine that Flight 93 is hijacked at around this time.[187]

9:29 AM—American 77 is now 35 miles west of the Pentagon, flying at 7,000 feet.

9:30 AM—Cleveland air controllers mistakenly conclude that Delta 1989 has been hijacked (History Commons)

9:30 AM—The transponder signal of United 93 ceases. At about this time, the plane apparently reverses direction and begins flying toward the capital.[188]

9:30 AM—Deena Burnett reports later that she received a call from husband, Thomas Burnett, Jr., alleged passenger on United 93.[189]

9:33 AM—FAA believes United 93 is a hijacked aircraft (History Commons)

9:34 AM—American 77 is now about 3.5 miles west-southwest of the Pentagon and starts a 330-degree descending right turn, bringing it to an altitude of about 2,000 feet four miles southwest of the Pentagon.[190]

---

[187] http://www.cnn.com/2001/US/09/16/inv.hijack.warning/
[188] http://911research.wtc7.net/planes/attack/flight93.html
[189] https://goo.gl/qcfZwv - as noted earlier, this is the source for all calls alleged from United 93
[190] http://goo.gl/u7R09E

9:36 AM—Sandra Bradshaw, flight attendant, allegedly calls United Airlines from United 93.[191]

9:36—Alice Hoagland later reports call at this time from son, Mark Bingham, alleged passenger on United 93.[192]

9:37 AM—American 77 allegedly crashes into the west side of the Pentagon, killing everyone on board and 125 people who were in the building.[193]

9:37 AM—Jeremy Glick later said to make call from United 93 at this time.[194]

9:37 AM—Thomas Burnett, Jr. later alleged to call residence from United 93 at this time.[195]

9:39-9:43—Lauren Grandcolas later reported to have made several calls during this time period from United 93.[196]

9:40 AM—Secretary of Transportation Mineta orders all planes to land.

---

[191] https://goo.gl/qcfZwv
[192] ibid
[193] http://en.wikipedia.org/wiki/American_Airlines_Flight_77
[194] https://goo.gl/qcfZwv
[195] ibid
[196] ibid

9:41 AM—Mark Bingham later alleged by his mother to have called a second time from United 93.

9:42 AM—Joseph DeLuca later reported to have made call from United 93.

9:43 AM—Joseph DeLuca later alleged second call from United 93.

9:43 AM—Todd Beamer reportedly calls GTE operator from United 93.

9:44 AM—Thomas Burnett, Jr. allegedly calls residence third time from United 93.

9:46 AM—Linda Gronlund allegedly calls from United 93.

9:47 AM—CeeCee Lyles, flight attendant, calls her residence from the ground, claiming to be on hijacked United 93.

9:49 AM—Marion Britton allegedly makes phone call from United 93.

9:49 AM—Sandra Bradshaw, flight attendant, allegedly calls residence from United 93.

9:52 AM—Sandra Bradshaw, flight attendant, allegedly calls residence again from United 93.[197]

---

[197] https://goo.gl/qcfZwv

9:53 AM—Honor Elizabeth Wainio allegedly calls her parents from United 93.[198]

9:58 AM—CeeCee Lyles, flight attendant, allegedly again calls her residence from United 93.[199]

9:58 AM—Edward Felt allegedly makes phone call from United 93.[200]

10:03 AM—United 93 crashes in a field in Shanksville, Pennsylvania, killing everyone on board.[201]

10:03-10:10 AM—United 93 "crashes" at Shanksville, PA (Official theory)

10:10 AM—ACARS message receipt shows United 93 still flying near Champaign, IL (Pilots for 9/11 Truth)

10:10 AM—The FAA orders all planes to land at nearest airports

10:15 AM—United acknowledges to employees that aircraft has landed near Jonestown, PA and "believed that this was Flight 93" (History Commons)

---

[198] ibid

[199] ibid

[200] ibid

[201] http://en.wikipedia.org/wiki/United_Airlines_Flight_93

10:17 AM—United Airlines notifies its employees of "crash" of Flight 93 (History Commons)

10:45 AM—Mystery plane arrives in Cleveland Airport. (Local Cleveland Media)

11:00 AM—Mayor White reports that a Boeing 767 made an emergency landing in Cleveland due to bomb threats. (No bomb was ever found.) He said the plane was going from Boston to Los Angeles.

11:26 AM—United Airlines publicly reports that Flight 93, en route from Newark, New Jersey, to San Francisco, has crashed in Pennsylvania, southeast of Pittsburgh.

11:43 AM—WCPO radio of Cincinnati posts an AP article that quotes Mayor White as identifying the aircraft as a Boeing 767 out of Boston. The article says that United had identified the plane as United 93. The AP quotes United as saying it was "deeply concerned" about United 175.[202]

11:53 AM—United Airlines confirms that Flight 175, from Boston to Los Angeles, has crashed

---

[202] http://goo.gl/3P0Fvt

with 56 passengers and nine crewmembers aboard.

ASK THE RIGHT QUESTIONS

Dean T. Hartwell

Using conclusions I have already derived, I have the small answers that lead to the big ones.

Q: Where did the planes go?

A: American 11 and American 77 did not fly anywhere. United 93 and United 175 flew west.

Q: Where did the United planes land?

A: United 93 was last tracked somewhere near Champaign, Illinois and United 175 was last tracked somewhere near Pittsburgh. No one knows where they landed.

Q: How near?

A: The ACARS records last show them in the vicinity of these cities, but without further information, there is no way to confirm a more accurate location. The main point is that they did not crash in Shanksville or New York City.

Q: What happened in Shanksville?

A: Agents of the government, acting upon reports of a crash, secured the area.

Q: Who were these agents?

A: People with authority.

Q: Such as?

A: The FBI. Given the reports of prior "terrorist" activity, the FBI could claim that Shanksville was a crime scene rather than a crash scene.

Q: What difference did that make?

A: Jurisdiction in a crash scene goes to the National Transportation Safety Board. Jurisdiction in a crime scene involving airplanes goes to the FBI.

Q: Was that unlawful of the FBI to do?

A: Not necessarily. They could claim reasonable belief a crime was committed. The main point is that people got to the scene and secured it quickly.

Q: OK. So what about allegations of eyewitnesses that United 93 was shot down?

A: They were wrong. United 93 flew west.

Q: How can we be sure that United 93 was really flying west?

A: We cannot be sure of anything. We go with the best evidence. The ACARS information was recorded contemporaneously and traced to the plane's serial number. This evidence places United 93 out west. The evidence that United 93 was shot down or that it crashed in Shanksville is meager, at best, and not based on contemporaneous information or specificity.

Q: Were there two United 93s?

A: Possibly. Flight numbers may duplicate. But serial numbers do not. Even the official theory says that United 93 had serial number N612UA.

Q: Could a second United 93 have crashed in Shanksville?

A: I suppose it is possible. It is more likely a ruse was created to make Shanksville look like a crash scene plausibly enough to get the public to believe it was United 93.

Q: So what happened to United 175?

A: The last ACARS could tell, it was headed west of Pittsburgh long after the "crash" in New York City. As with United 93, we need more information to be specific.

Q: Then what hit the second World Trade Center tower?

A: That's a leading question.

Q: Do we know that anything hit the World Trade Center?

A: No.

Q: Lots of witnesses said they saw a plane hit WTC2. Were they wrong?

A: Eyewitness evidence is often shaky. The witnesses could have been mistaken or they could have been planted.

Q: Planted witnesses? Wouldn't someone have talked by now?

A: If someone did talk, they would not likely be believed.

Q: Why is that?

A: The public has already bought the idea that planes hit the towers. The official narrative has long set in and cannot be undone by someone talking.

Q: Has this sort of thing happened before?

A: Yes.   Members of the Navy, including James Stockdale, admitted many years after the Gulf of Tonkin incident that we had instigated the conflict there.

Q: How is that significant?

A: If the public knew at the time that the story of a North Vietnamese attack was a ruse, it might not have favored escalating the war there.

Q: Will we get the truth about the Towers someday?

A: If we do, it will be too late to do any good. The main point is that we need to be wary of government lies *when they tell them to us.*

Q: Ok.   How about the American flights? What happened to the plane for American 11?

A: The evidence that it remained on the runway is stronger than the evidence that it took off. The original Bureau of Transportation Statistics shows it was never scheduled and that it never flew. None of the plane parts were found at the World Trade Center.   And the article by "loopDloop" quotes an airline agent admitting in an early report that the plane remained parked near the gate it would allegedly take off from.

Q: Is there any chance American 11 flew but was simply not recorded?

A: I suppose there is a chance, but not a good one. For one thing, it would be quite a coincidence that one of four flights alleged to have been hijacked would just happen not to have statistics recorded for it.

Q: There is a report that someone spotted American 11 in the air. Is there anything to that?

A: No. The flight on which someone allegedly saw it was United 175! That is hardly independent corroboration given the fraud we know about United 175!

Q: Wouldn't someone have noticed that plane that was to be used for American 11 was still parked?

A: That is not likely. By the time anyone would have thought about American 11, the public had already gotten the news that American 11 struck World Trade Center One. And it is highly unlikely that anyone could have matched the flight with any identification number. From the outside, it looked just like any other plane at the airport. Also, because of the Secretary of Transportation and Federal Aviation Administration orders for planes to land, there were probably a large number of planes around.

Q: What eventually happened to all the planes involved?

A: I don't know. It would make sense if someone eventually destroyed these planes or at least disguised them.

Q: Did anything strike the Pentagon?

A: All I can say about this is that United 77 did not hit the Pentagon.

Q: What happened to the plane for United 77?

A: It most likely remained parked somewhere. The plotters may have used the air phone from it, but the plane did not fly that day.

Q: What about the passengers?

A: There were no passengers.

Q: What about the alleged passengers?

A: Consider who alleged that there were passengers.

Q: The media showed lists of people it said were on the planes.

A: Yes, the media said that.

Q: Were the alleged passengers real people?

A: Some of them apparently were.

Q: Why do you say "apparently"?

A: There is no way to prove or disprove who was real and who was not.

Q: What about relatives who have come forward and talked about people who were on the list?

A: That is *evidence* of the reality of a person. But it does not prove it.

Q: Why not?

A: There are other reasonable explanations as to why a person would make this claim.

Q: Like what?

A: They could be paid to do so. They could also be mistaken.

Q: Mistaken?

A: They could believe that a relative was on one of the planes. But they could have been given false information. The relative could be somewhere else.

Q: That possibility would make the person real, wouldn't it?

A: Yes it would. It would suggest the person in question was not the type of person they were perceived to be.

Q: Why don't we check an objective source which specializes in this type of information?

A: There is no such thing.

Q: How about the Social Security Death Index?

A: The SSDI is reliable when one looks up someone they actually knew. The listing is corroborated. Not so with names of people that one has not previously even heard of.

Q: How reliable is the SSDI for the alleged passengers of 9/11?

A: It is not reliable at all.

Q: Why is that?

A: Roughly half of the alleged passengers are listed on the SSDI. This simply means that some names on the passenger lists were REPORTED to the Social Security Administration as having died that day.

Q: Does that prove that those were names of real people?

A: No. It simply means someone purporting to be a relative contacted the Administration with a Social Security Number.

Q: Did anyone report seeing anybody standing at the gates of any of the alleged flights?

A: No.

Q: Why does that matter?

A: It allows the plotters an easier hand at adjusting take-off times so as to make the phone calls "fit" into the "flights."

Q.   What do you mean by that?

A.   Consider that Flight 11 allegedly struck the World Trade Center at 8:46 a.m. EST and that Flight 175 allegedly struck the south tower at 9:03 a.m.[203]

Q: OK.

A: United 93 "officially" took off at 8:44 a.m.

Q: OK.

A: The plotters got the public to believe that the United 93 passengers confronted hijackers. To get us to believe that, it helped to also believe that passengers were having phone calls with relatives who advised them of what had happened at the World Trade Center.

Q: Are there reports of relatives calling the passengers?

A: Yes. Several relatives reported making calls to the alleged passengers telling them about the alleged crashes at the World Trade Center (Alleged Flights 11 and 175) and the Pentagon (Alleged Flight 77).[204]

---

[203] http://goo.gl/dSOJqG
[204] http://goo.gl/5we2sl

Q: So, what do the reports of calls have to do with the departure time for United 93?

A: United 93's scheduled time was 8:00 a.m. The public could not be expected to know about the World Trade Center until a little after 9:00, when the second alleged strike was shown live on national television. The alleged hijacking on United 93 began at 9:28 a.m.[205]

Q: When did United 93 actually take off?

A: The Bureau of Transportation Statistics, the most reliable information because of its contemporaneous manner of collecting data, shows United 93 as having taken off at 8:28.

Q: So, the official 8:44 time represented a delay that the official story would later need?

A: Right. Recall the scheduled departure time was 8:00. It would be hard to believe that the hijacking would start 1 hour and 20 minutes into the flight.

Q: Why is that a problem?

A: The storyline set up ahead of time has United 93 going on a fairly straight path west from Newark. The "hijack" is set up to occur

---

[205] http://goo.gl/kJ3awL

before the plane makes a direction turn near Cleveland at around 9:30 AM.

Q: The "hijack" time was set up ahead of time?

A: Almost everything was.

Q: Almost? What times were left open?

A: The "events" for which it was possible to leave open. The departure times could be established through the media because no one is likely to contradict it. No one understood the significance of any of these "flights" at the time of their take-offs and alleged take-offs.

Q: Back to United 93. It seems there were two times available – the Bureau of Transportation Statistics at 8:28 AM and the media reports of 8:44 AM. Why not use 8:28 AM for the official theory?

A: The 8:44 AM departure time works better because it allows 44 minutes for the "hijack" to start, which is plausible. More importantly, the hijack time of 9:28 allows the so-called passengers adequate time to learn of the other "hijackings" on the other "flights."

Q: How do you mean?

A: The public did not learn of the World Trade Center crashes until about 9:00. The relatives' calls to passengers and passenger calls to relatives had to fit in after this time but not too much later than 9:28 as "hijacker" actions would be too loud and noticeable to be ignored.[206]

Q: OK. But what about the 8:28 AM "wheels off" departure time?

A: With an 8:28 flight, the "hijack" would have occurred over an hour after departure. The plausibility of the official story gets strained the longer the plane takes to make its turn at Cleveland. A hijack after that turn makes no sense because the turn marked a diversion from the flight path.

Q: Why didn't those who put together the official story just go with 8:28 AM?

A: They may well have feared the risk of placing the hijacking too late as too much of a risk.

---

[206] The first reported call about a hijacking on United 93 was allegedly received by Deena Burnett from husband Tom, alleged passenger at 9:27 AM. She said watch could have been a minute or two off. See http://www.911myths.com/index.php/United_Airlines_Flight_93_Tim eline

Q: So how did they get 8:44 AM to work?

A: They put a story through the media about the long wait in line for the plane before it was cleared for take-off.[207]

Q: So, what is the real significance of the script telling us that relatives warned anyone about what happened to the other "flights"?

A: Without those warnings, which allegedly started just a few minutes after the first Burnett call, there is no story about heroic passengers prepared to fight suicide hijackers, a meme used as propaganda to rally the call for war.

Q: So, what else was done to create the official story?

A: The plotters needed help in creating an illusion of crashed planes, hijackings, and passenger phone calls.

Q: OK. Did those people later said to be passengers help the plotters?

A: To answer that, one needs to know who the plotters were.

---

[207] http://goo.gl/2EKLxK

Q: OK, who were they?

A: A group willing and able to create an illusion in order to direct public outrage against innocent people.

Q: I agree that that is what happened—but how do the alleged passengers fit into this?

A: To make an illusion work, plotters must convince the audience (the public) that the illusion is real. They cast a shadow over the truth while they construct their lies.

Q: So? What has that got to do with the alleged passengers?

A: To create the illusion of crashed commercial planes, the plotters, among other things, planted personal effects at the crash sites.[208]

Q: Where did they get these personal effects?

A: The same place one usually gets another's personal effects - from the people who owned the effects. This could have happened by theft, coercion or agreement.

---

[208] http://www.rense.com/general68/mrev.htm

Some of the effects were likely counterfeit, given that few "passengers" really participated.

Q: Were the alleged passengers a part of the plot?

A: That depends upon the plot to which you refer.

Q: What do you mean?

A: Only the plotters knew the whole picture about the plot and the outcome.

Q: So what did the alleged passengers know?

A: Only what they were told. No one could be trusted to know too much about the plot because (a) that is risky and (b) unnecessary.

Q: What were they told?

A: They were told where and when to show up on that morning, they were told not to bring anyone, and some were told to make phone calls.

Q: How does that make them a part of the big plot?

A: It doesn't. They could have been told they were needed for an important project and that it had to do with national security.

Q: What was their agenda?

A: They believed that their help was needed and that secrecy was required to help the people in whom they placed their trust.

Q: How many of them were there?

A: Only the ones who were necessary to perpetuate this hoax, which is not too many. It could have been as few as twenty.

Q: Why twenty?

A: That is the reported number of passengers who made phone calls from the "planes."[209]

Q: How many people boarded United 93 and United 175?

A: No passengers. For all we know, the two planes could have been lifted off and directed from the ground.

---

[209] http://911research.wtc7.net/planes/evidence/phonecalls.html

Q: What happened to the so-called passengers?

A: A couple of possibilities.

Q: What are my choices?

A: You could guarantee their silence by killing them OR

Q: Or what?

A: Keep them hidden for future assistance.

Q: What does that mean?

A: They could be agents who work on different operations. They would be available to help with a future operation.

Q: Who was behind this operation?

A: To answer that, it is important to identify the ingredients to this operation that made it work effectively.

Q: What were the ingredients?

A: Intelligence was one. The plotters had to know what was scheduled to happen when. They had to know what planes were supposed to take off from what city to what city, for instance. United 93 was flying for the first time on a Tuesday that day. And several of the "passengers" were originally scheduled to fly on a later flight, United 91.[210]

Q: Who has this type of intelligence?

A: Certain people have intelligence, or information not known to the public. They need not belong to an agency, like the CIA. But they develop connections, or confidences with other people who give them information.

Q: Who are they?

A: They don't have a sign on their face and their place of employment will not necessarily reveal them to you. Typically, the organizations for whom they work give them high security clearances.

Q: How do they earn this?

A: Reputation. They become known as people who do not reveal secrets.

Q: How do you know this?

---

[210] http://911review.org/inn.globalfreepress/First-Flight-93.html

A: Because that is the way anyone obtains information not generally known. It involves protecting the source of the information.

Q: So one ingredient is intelligence via people who keep secrets?

A: Yes.

Q: What is another ingredient?

A: Persuasion.

Q: How is that?

A: People who can persuade other people to do something without necessarily telling them what the overall plan is.

Q: How does one identify such persuaders?

A: They have authority or the ability to coerce, or both.

Q: What type of authority?

A: Legal authority. Like the FBI agents who showed up at Shanksville and the Pentagon and who began to control the investigation at the scene. They could persuade others to either enter the crime scene or leave it, depending on the level of trust they felt towards those people.

Q: Do those with legal authority have to believe they are acting legally?

A: No, but it helps.

Q: Why is that?

A: They are not likely to have anything to confess to anyone else.

Q: What if they do?

A: A person who coerces others could be called upon to persuade, perhaps with threats.

Q: What would be an example of that?

A: Whoever ran the DNA "tests" that supposedly matched remains from the "crash" sites to relatives was likely coerced to "fix" the matches.   And those who planted personal effects at the scenes.

Q: What was another ingredient?

A: Access.

Q: What do you mean by that?

A: Someone had to convince those who follow flights on screens that American 11 and American 77 really flew and that United 93 and United 175 really flew back east.   And transcripts of flight observers and pilots had to be manufactured. This takes access to those screens and transcripts.

Q: Who could gain that access?

A: At the very least someone at the airlines would have had to provide help. And some people with computer savvy.

Q: Any other ingredients?

A: Discretion, confidence and the ability to cover up or minimize any mistakes. And one more thing.

Q: What is that?

A: Communication with the media. The intelligence people probably handled that aspect of the operation.

Q: How do you know that?

A: Because the media gathers intelligence and filters what their corporate bosses will allow them to say.

Q: OK. I have the ingredients down. Who put these ingredients together?

A: You mean the names of people?

Q: Yes. What were the names of the people who masterminded this operation?

A: They don't have names. They work in the shadows and they pull the strings of people like the occupants of the White House and Congress. They use coercion and encourage the occupants to use authority.

Q: What was the purpose of this operation?

A: To draw the United States into wars in the Middle East fighting for a cause everyone would agree was worthy. The events of 9/11, as reported to the public, served as a match to light the fires of war.

Q: Was this unusual?

A: No. Most wars start with lies. I mentioned the Gulf of Tonkin and Viet Nam earlier. The first Bush Administration used lies from the daughter of a Kuwaiti ambassador to sell the first war against Iraq. Later the second Bush Administration would lie about weapons of mass destruction. So, lying to provoke a war is actually common.

Q: Will it happen again?

A: It could.

Q: What can we do if it does?

A: Ask questions as early as you can. Someday the public may take notice that all wars are phony.

Q: OK. What about the pilots and the flight crew?

A: There is something about the way in which they got their assignments that should tell us something.

Q: What do you mean?

A: Half of the pilots and most of the crew got their assignments shortly before 9/11.[211] In many cases, they "bumped" other people who had signed up to work the flights

Q: What does that tell us?

A: It tells us that the selection of personnel was done carefully, in such a manner that

---

[211] http://goo.gl/b27OyC

those who were "bumped" did not have much of a chance to figure out why they were bumped. It also gave no one any time to make any connections about the pilots and crew members suddenly asked to work.

Q: Why were the others bumped?

A: They did not fit into the plot. The "right" pilots and crew, those who would work the simulations, got into position.

Q: What did the alleged pilots and crew know?

A: No more than what was necessary.

Q: Where are they now?

A: Like the passengers, most of them were fictitious. In a plot where flights are faked, who needs pilots and crew members?

Q: Why are 3,000 people reported as having died at the World Trade Center that day?

A: To understand best what happened, we could review the story starting from the end and proceed backwards.

The outcome of the story is that the deaths of approximately 3,000 people were reported by the media and by representatives of the federal and state governments of the United States of America. Most of the public apparently believed this assertion to be true, as evidenced by polls and the frequent sighting of United States flags in public.

Q: What caused the media and government to report the massive number of deaths?

A: The ostensible cause stemmed from prior reports of four hijacked airplanes, all of which were flown by terrorists into buildings or the ground.

Q: Where did the report of the deaths come from?

A: The total number of deaths reported came from information revealed by government and media sources as to the number of occupants of the four airplanes in question and the number of people reported dead from the fall of the World Trade Centers 1 and 2 and the Pentagon.

Q: Who gave the public the names of the supposed victims?

A: Official and media sources[212] compiled the names of victims at the World Trade Center.

Q: Where did they get the names?

A: According to author Joel Best, "The names came from firms who offered lists of employees thought to have been in the buildings and from worried friends and family members…"[213]

Q: Who were the companies that occupied the World Trade Center?

A: The occupancy of the World Trade Center buildings 1 and 2 was mysterious. Many floors in these buildings went UNLEASED from the birth of the WTC in 1972 until 1998, according to records from a Freedom of Information Act request.[214] It is unknown how many of the floors were actually used by real companies.

Q: Why is this significant?

---

[212] http://goo.gl/IIJIGz

[213] Best, Joel. *More Damned Lies and Statistics: How Numbers Confuse Public Issues*, University of California Press, 2004, 109.

[214] http://letsrollforums.com/press-release-world-trade-t24256.html

A: It leaves open the possibility that fictitious companies could have generated fictitious victims. They could have done this in a short period of time (1998-2001) to attract little attention.

Q: What else about the companies at the World Trade Center stands out?

A: A handful of companies owned several floors.[215]

Q: Why does that matter?

A: This fact explains the ease with which knowledge of the victim fraud could be known to relatively few people.

Q: Did people jump out of the towers?

A: No. Faked photos and video footage showed people jumping from the towers.[216]

Q: So what if this was faked?

A: There should be no need for fakery if people really died. No official sources

---

[215] Ibid
[216] http://goo.gl/Yb1i5T

denounced this fraud, which was used to help sell the "War on Terror."

Q: How was it determined who got money for injuries or for family member deaths?

A: On September 21, 2001, Congress debated and passed the Air Transportation Safety and System Stabilization Act (ATSSSA), Public Law 107-42.[217] Those who filed claims under this law as people injured in the attacks or family members of those killed, had to waive all rights to sue for damages against ANYONE.

A total of 2,880 family members filed a claim, for which the Fund paid out $8.5 billion.[218]

Q: Why was the waiver put in place?

A: The government wanted few lawsuits, where ugly truths could come out, namely the secret that the victims were frauds. A tidy two or three million dollars could go a long way to buy silence.

---

[217] Hadfield, Gillian K. "Framing the Choice between Cash and the Courthouse: Experiences with the 9/11 Victim Compensation Fund;" USC Center in Law, Economics and Organization, page 7.
[218] Ibid, page 9.

Q: What about reports of bodies at the World Trade Center and DNA testing used to identify some people?

A: Anyone can report a body. Anyone can claim DNA testing was done. A better question is whether anyone WITNESSED a person dying or if anyone could explain how they identified matter at the scene as part of a specific person.

Q: What about phone calls from the towers?

A: They are as real as the phone calls from the so-called flights.

Dean T. Hartwell

Was 9/11 a Movie?

Dean T. Hartwell

The events of 9/11 played to the public on television screens with searing images of towers falling and people who made scripted statements to media figures like Larry King. From this point of view, the plot, the actors and the message are easy to discern.

If we follow the script closely, we may well identify those responsible for its production. If history does indeed repeat itself, we can stop them from the next big deception.

PLOT

A group of people, known as the "Elite," sit in golden chairs in a mansion and agree that the United States needs to get into a war in order to improve the stocks of companies they own.

The Elite decide to invent a pretext for the war. They study previous uses of pretext, including the lies used to start the Viet Nam War, and agree to create a phony terrorist attack and to blame it on "Muslim extremists."

They contact leading politicians and friends in the media and persuade them to begin blaming Osama bin Laden, a CIA asset, for terrorism. The politicians and media also start using a phrase "al Qaeda" frequently to refer to bin Laden's followers.

The Elite hires carefully chosen television contacts to secretly write and produce a movie for release on television on September 11, 2001. They tell the contacts to make the movie appear to be a real terrorist attack on United States soil.

Instead of casting calls, which would draw too much public attention, the contacts call upon a few friends in the intelligence world to play the roles of passengers and airline attendants on hijacked planes.

They select others to act as though they received phone calls and to be prepared on the day of the movie's release to speak to the media contacts and the FBI about those calls.

A spectacular actual demolition of three towers of the World Trade Center, great special effects like fake planes and false images of jumpers and the mediocre acting of the phone callers and phone call recipients convince the public that a terrorist attack has taken the lives of about 3,000 people.

The movie, simply called "9/11," receives more of an audience than anything before on television.

(All scenes depicting the Elite mysteriously disappear before the movie showing. It is alleged that Vice President Dick Cheney took these portions of the movie to an undisclosed location, promising to reveal them in seventy-five years.)

ACTORS

A few actors receive starring roles for on-screen performance. Betty Ong plays an airline attendant who speaks calmly for four minutes telling her airline about a hijacking, a stabbing and mace used on her flight. The audience never hears the remaining twenty minutes of her conversation, an oversight not fully explained.

Ted Olson acts as the Solicitor General of the United States. Just hours after his wife dies on one of the flights, he talks to Larry King about how he talked to his wife on the flight and how brave she was. When Olson, panned for a shaky performance, keeps changing his mind about what phone she used, his character marries a woman who looks like his wife!

Lisa Jefferson plays a phone attendant supervisor who receives a phone call so sensitive that one of her employees hands the phone to Jefferson in a panic. Jefferson captures the hearts of the audience by speaking to a man on one of the doomed flights.

Jefferson mourns the man's passing and ensures his place in history by quoting him in pure Patrick Henry ("give me liberty or give me death") form as having said "Let's Roll" before attacking the hijackers. The widow of the man, Lisa Beamer, meets with Jefferson and they become friends.

Politicians of all stripes put aside their differences and call for a perpetual "War on Terror."

MESSAGE

The movie receives near-universal praise for its simple message "You are either with us or against us." A vague message of how terrible evil is and how we must all work together to defeat it comes across clearly.

Critics point out the flaws in the movie script. "How could passengers make cell phone calls at those heights?" they asked. "Where is the plane that crashed into the Pentagon?" And many other questions.

For these comments, the critics earn the sarcastic nickname "9/11 truthers." This group makes numerous movies and documentaries of their own, but the powers that be on television, close friends of the Elite, never show them. One powerful contact is quoted as saying "Let those truthers write books. No one reads them, anyway."

Dean T. Hartwell

AFTERWORD

Dean T. Hartwell

Even if I am completely accurate in my account of the events of 9/11, there will be no reward for it. The United States government, the media, and others who prop up the lies about this and other recent events in history are an institution designed to thwart such truths.

The lies in turn serve to justify so much about our society that we take for granted. They justify our defense (i.e., phony war) budget that in turn props up defense contractors and the sunshine patriots who scream bloody murder at the slightest provocation.

Too many jobs are on the line for any change in this order:

- national security, airport security, homeland security
- emergency preparedness and others who fear a nation without fear
- the political pundits who gain status by appearing to be "tough" instead of sensible
- politicians who know no other social order except to yell at an enemy the loudest

- and the rest of us, who are too afraid to be identified as "unpatriotic" or "foolish" if we speak our minds.

So, this concludes my tenth book, nine of which I have published over the last six years. I write at a manic pace because that is my style. I will now go into hibernation from writing and can be reached at my web site.[219]

The world will continue to spin in the interim. Similar hoaxes and government lies will continue. And the public will continue to go along with it.

The public isn't as gullible as it used to be. But the "tipping point," when people will take action to change a government that misrepresents itself, is miles away.

Why is that?

We perceive that we have too much to lose if we revolt. We are too heavily invested in the persistent dream that if we simply work hard, we can achieve what we want.

Successful revolutions happen when people have nothing to lose. When they have so little

---

[219] http://deanhartwell.weebly.com

to begin with, it is much easier to get someone to lead the way and get others to follow.

Don't wait for a revolution. It ain't gonna happen.

But don't lose hope altogether. Had we known on September 11, 2001 what we know now about the day's events, the plotters would have stood out in the same light that they hid from. When the public finally reads the script, justice may yet prevail at last.

killtown.blogspot.com/2007

letsrollforums.com

Serendipity.li

theage.com.au

therealnewsonline.com

INDEX

---

[220] I know Indexes usually go with last name first, but the reader should find this short index easy to use. I never was much for conformity.

Printed in Great Britain
by Amazon